# A Century of

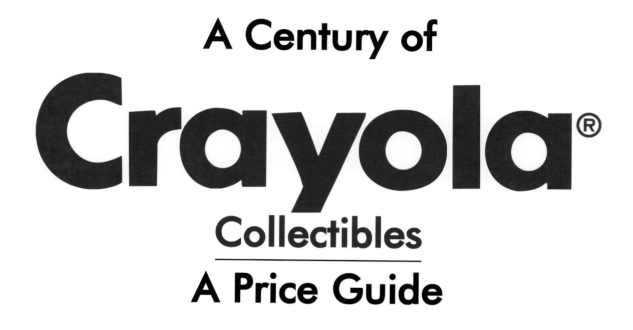

# Crayola®
## Collectibles
## A Price Guide

Bonnie B. Rushlow

Photographs by Courtney R. Rushlow
(unless otherwise noted)

Published by  Hobby House Press, Inc.
Grantsville, Maryland
www.hobbyhouse.com

# Dedication

To my husband, Ken, and our daughters, Whitney and Courtney, who have supported and contributed to my Crayola® obsession throughout the years. Thanks for your love, encouragement and patience!

Crayola, Clayola, Staonal, Artista, Artista II, Silly Putty, The Crayola FACTORY, So Big, Dream-Makers, An-Du-Septic, Clay Time, Kids First, Classpack, Anti-Roll, Anti-Dust, Model Magic, Peacock, Portfolio, Tempratone, the crayon character "Tip," chevron* and serpentine** designs are registered trademarks; Construction Paper and rainbow/swash*** are trademarks of Binney & Smith, used with permission.

The contents of this book represent the work of the named author, are copyright by the author and are not approved or sponsored by Binney & Smith Inc. Binney & Smith Inc. is not responsible for any errors or omissions or for any opinions expressed in this book.

*Chevron design: The green and yellow V-shaped design on the front and back of a box of Crayola® Crayons and other products.

**Serpentine design: This is a distinct winding, bending and twisting line design located at each end of the label on Crayola® Crayons and other products.

***Rainbow/swash design: The design with the word "CRAYOLA®" and a "swash of rainbow" under it.

**Cover:**
Front: Assorted Boxes of Crayola® Crayons.
Back: Crayola® Crayon United States Postal Service Stamp, "Celebrate the Century" Series, 1998. *Photograph courtesy of Binney & Smith.*

Additional copies of this book may be purchased at $24.95 (plus postage and handling) from
**Hobby House Press, Inc.**
1 Corporate Drive, Grantsville, MD 21536
1-800-554-1447
**www.hobbyhouse.com**
or from your favorite bookstore or dealer.

Printed in the United States of America

ISBN: 0-87588-638-8

# Table of Contents

# Acknowledgments

I wish to thank the following individuals for their many contributions to my Crayola® collection and to this book:

- My daughter, Courtney, for the countless hours she spent taking photographs of my collection.

- Ken, for all his assistance with this project.

- My mother, Edith Bond, who bought me my first box of Crayola® Crayons and encouraged me to use my imagination.

- My sister, Judy Hansard, who has contributed some of the most unique and interesting Crayola® "toys" to my collection.

- My editor, Virginia Ann Heyerdahl, who not only did a wonderful job of making sure that all my i's were dotted and t's crossed, but also for the skillful and professional manner in which she completed this project.

- Theresa Black, Mark Brown, Gary Ruddell, Sherry White, Brenda Wiseman and Lisa Zuckerman at Hobby House Press, Inc., for offering me the opportunity to write this book and for ensuring that its publication became a reality.

- Diana Sparrow and Binney & Smith, the Crayola® people, for allowing us copyright permission to publish this book on my favorite topic.

- Sharon Sanford, my new Crayola® pal, who spent a great deal of time and energy photographing items from her collection to include in this book.

- Beverly Robinson, a wonderful art teacher, fellow crayon collector and "best pal" – thanks for your friendship and encouragement, and for always being there for me.

- Diane Owens, my favorite antiquing buddy, who first introduced me to eBay and who travels far and wide looking for that rare Crayola® box or tin.

- Barbara Crews, the ultimate collector, who introduced me to Sherry White and Hobby House Press, Inc.

- Darrel Irwin, who shared his unique miniatures that he makes from actual Crayola® Crayon boxes.

- Ron DeLong, Gail Farrell, Mickey Myers and Kate Nessler for allowing me to use photographs of their artwork in this publication. Also, to Janet Swahn of ART4SALE, who assisted me in purchasing an original Tony Azzito painting.

- Dr. Eldon Katter, the editor of *School Arts* magazine, who entrusted me with his copies of *The Drawing Teacher* and *The Art Educationist*.

- Reuben Jackson and other staff members at the Smithsonian Archives who assisted with my research on Binney & Smith.

- My many, many fellow Crayola® collectors who have helped me gather information for this book: Jerry Jaffee, Charlie Martin, Marianne Meyer, Karen Mazzarese, Jason Forman (thecrayonman), Lori Read, Dianne Ross, Gary Schroeder, Phil Stevens and others. Thanks to each of you for sharing your expertise and for the friendly competition along the way.

- And last, but not least, thanks to my many other friends and colleagues who have given me encouragement, as well as a bunch of Crayola® "stuff" throughout the years – you are the best!

# Part I: Collecting Crayola® Crayons

## Introduction

**Most of us can remember** opening that new green and yellow box of Crayola® Crayons on the first day of school. The distinctive and familiar smell of those brand-new waxy crayons is one that brings back long-forgotten childhood memories. In fact, according to a study by Yale University, the scent of Crayola® Crayons is among the 20 most recognizable to American adults.

**Why would anyone want to collect Crayola® Crayons?** And how can the value of these interesting collectibles be determined? In this book, the author will provide the answers to these questions, as well as offer information about the history of the Binney & Smith Company, a chronology of changes made in crayon colors and packaging through the years, descriptions and current values, and other interesting facts and trivia about Crayola® Crayons.

**Collecting Crayola® Crayons** may not be among the most popular hobbies, but it can be a very rewarding one. There are numerous Crayola® items and other Binney & Smith memorabilia that can be collected. Of course, the most common and recognizable is the green and yellow box of Crayola® Crayons, but there are many other collectibles as well. Some of these include early Binney & Smith distinctive tins and boxes of crayons, chalks and paints. In addition, collectors today can find artwork, toys, games, puzzles and an array of other products with the familiar serpentine and chevron designs, as well as the newer Crayola® rainbow/swash trademark.

Three boxes of eight Crayola® Crayons, all No. 8. The box on the left is "School Crayons" and the other two are "Different Brilliant Colors." Only the box in the middle is noted as "Non-Toxic." *Photograph courtesy of Sharon Sanford.*

# Determining the Value

**As most collectors know,** assigning a value to their collectibles can be difficult and often misleading. So, how can the true value of a box of crayons be determined? Many factors influence the dollar amount attached to any given item. For example, a very old Crayola® box may be practically worthless if it is badly worn, stained, torn or missing the original crayons. On the other hand, a rare box of crayons in mint condition may be priced at hundreds of times its original value. (Remember, the first box of Crayola® Crayons sold for only a nickel!) Even an extremely worn item may be valuable if it is a "one-of-a-kind" collectible!

**Considering the popularity of Crayola®** Crayons, the more common objects are not too difficult to locate. Old boxes of crayons can often be found at flea markets, antique malls, yard and estate sales, and in attics across America. In addition, the Internet is an excellent source for locating information about Crayola® products, prices and sources. For the serious collector, eBay is an excellent way to obtain the hard-to-find and most sought-after items.

**Through the years, Crayola®** Crayons have been packaged in tiny boxes with a few small crayons to large boxes of 120 crayons containing every conceivable color. Crayon, chalk and paint tins are also extremely collectible items and can be found in a variety of shapes, sizes and colors. Vintage paint and crayon tins in cylindrical containers are scarce and often harder to find. Of course, this makes them even more desirable – especially if they are in mint condition.

**In this reference book,** you will note that the range of prices will vary between the lowest and highest, depending on factors such as age, condition and availability of the item. As most avid collectors and "eBayers" know, sellers who are not familiar with a product may ask an exorbitant amount for a frequently found item. Conversely, an extremely rare or unusual item may have a relatively inexpensive price tag. Buyers should research each item carefully and be aware of both extremes.

An assortment of Binney & Smith products.

A box of 16 Crayola® Crayons in mint condition.

# Determining the Grade

**As with any collectible,** a box of Crayola® Crayons can be graded according to its condition. Vintage boxes and tins with clear graphics and few imperfections are among the most desirable and valued by crayon collectors. Collectors should take care to examine the crayons, as well as the box or tin in which they are contained. Of course, a box of unused crayons with the original paper labels intact is much more valuable than one with missing or broken crayons or crayons with no labels.

**Crayola® collectors should** always ask questions about the condition of an item before deciding whether or not to purchase it. Although the vendor may attempt to provide an accurate description, he or she may not have the expertise to do so. Determining the grade of a particular item may be difficult for the non-collector. Therefore, to avoid possible deception and disappointment, it is very important that the buyer make any specific inquiries about the item prior to its purchase.

**In an effort to provide consistency** in determining the condition of a particular item, the following grading system may be useful in helping to determine the general condition of crayon boxes and tins. It is important to remember that the grade of an item has nothing to do with its age. Whether a pristine box of Crayola® Crayons is dated 1903 or 2003, it will be described as being in "mint" condition.

 **Mint:** The item is flawless with no wear, tears, dents, scratches, stains, damage or imperfections of any kind. Vintage items in mint condition are extremely rare and usually bring top dollar due to their perfect condition. Mint-condition items are often still sealed in cellophane or other original wrappers.

 **MIB:** Stands for "Mint-in-Box" and is sometimes used to identify a box of crayons that has been rarely or never removed from its original package.

 **Near Mint:** The item may not be flawless, but is very close to perfect. The box or tin may have a few very minor dents or other small imperfections. All crayons are present and unused with wrappers totally intact.

 **Excellent:** The item is in very nice condition, but may have a few imperfections. These may be minor, such as a crease or small worn area on the box or tin in an inconspicuous place. All crayons are present and labels are intact; crayons may have been used very little, if at all.

 **Very Good:** The item has been used and shows some wear, but it is still worth collecting and displaying. A few crayons may be used or missing, or there may be torn or missing labels; however, the box or tin is clean, intact and relatively undamaged.

 **Good:** The item has been used and shows a moderate amount of wear and tear. There may be stains, scratches, dents or other obvious signs of use. Crayons may be missing, broken or not the original ones that came in the box or tin. The box or tin is worn and graphics may be somewhat faded or difficult to read, but it is still nice enough to display.

**Fair:** The item has a great deal of wear and tear. There may be major scratches and/or dents, stains, tears and other damage. Most of the crayons are missing, broken, melted or not the original ones that came in the box or tin. The box or tin is extremely scratched, worn and graphics are faded and difficult to read. This grade is considered inferior by most collectors and is, most likely, not one worthy of displaying.

 **Poor:** The item is extremely worn and shows a great deal of abuse. There are numerous scratches, dents, stains, tears and other obvious imperfections. All of the crayons are missing, broken or melted. The box or tin is in major disrepair and/or unusable condition. A collector might consider purchasing an item with this grade if it is a "one-of-a-kind" item or if some part of the item can be salvaged to use with another box or tin in the collection. For example, a crayon that is rare or in good condition might be used to complete a box or tin that is in very good shape.

Remember that not all collectors use the same grading system. Therefore, it is important that the buyer carefully consider the descriptions, pictures and other available information before finalizing a sale. This will ultimately help to ensure fewer problems and greater satisfaction with your Crayola® purchase.

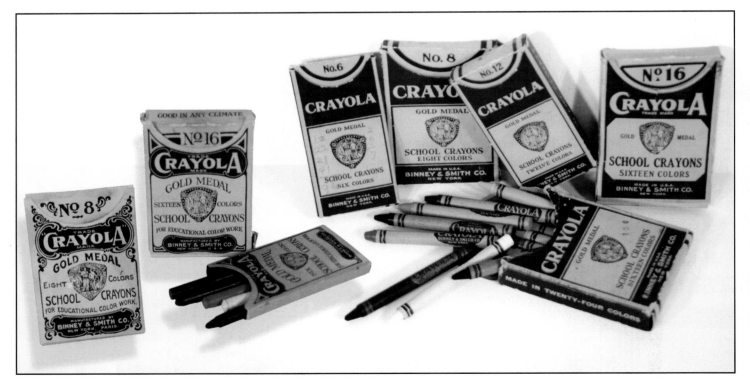

Vintage boxes of Crayola® Crayons in good to fair condition.

## Chapter 1

# In the Beginning. . .

The first crayons that resembled the sticks that we call "crayons" today were thought to have originated in Europe and were probably made of charcoal and oil. The charcoal was later replaced by various hues of powdered pigments. The discovery of substituting wax for the oil in the mixture produced sticks that were stronger and easier to handle. While these discoveries were being made in Europe, the foundation was being laid for a company that would turn the crayon into its best-known product in the United States; one that would reach the households of generations of children throughout the world.

The colorful history of Crayola® Crayons began over a hundred years ago with two cousins from very diverse backgrounds. In 1860, C. Harold Smith was born in London, England. Four years later, on the other side of the Atlantic Ocean, his uncle, Joseph Binney, started a small chemical company in Peekskill, New York.

In England during this period of history, the law required that a family's estate be inherited and managed by the eldest son. Although his family was originally well-to-do, Harold knew that it was very unlikely that he would ever see any of the

Peekskill Chemical Works. *Photograph courtesy of Binney & Smith.*

family fortune. As the youngest of eight children, he was taken out of school when his father fell on hard times and was apprenticed to a tradesman at the age of thirteen. When he was fifteen, Harold's father sent him to New Zealand, one of the distant colonies of the British Empire where youngest sons were often sent to live. The journey, which took 180 days, was miserable. Food was scarce; rodents and insects were plentiful.

When he arrived in New Zealand, young Harold was sent into the jungle with a logging crew. As a result of an accident, he became separated from the rest of the crew and ended up spending several months living among the savage Maoris before finding his way back to civilization. At the age of sixteen, Harold sailed across the Pacific to San Francisco in the steerage of a tramp steamer. He made his way east on the newly completed Union Pacific Railway – sometimes he paid the fare; other times he hitched a ride in cabooses.

A red barn. *Photograph courtesy of Binney & Smith.*

In 1876, he arrived in New York City. After spending some time in the dirty noisy city, he decided to travel up the Hudson River to visit his uncle, Joseph Binney, at his small plant in Peekskill. At the Peekskill Chemical Works, Binney made products such as lampblack by burning whale oil.

After a week's visit, Joseph Binney gave his adventurous young nephew the money for a ticket back to England. When Harold arrived in London, he found many friends, but had little money. He soon became a door-to-door salesman, selling fine horsehair for making violin bows and other useful products. Harold ended up earning so much money that he decided to take a vacation to Paris, where he promptly spent every penny he possessed. When his family finally located him through a detective, Harold returned home to London. There he was given three things: a lecture, a ticket to America and a five-pound note to start his new life.

Although Harold found different odd jobs

when he arrived back in New York, he could no longer afford his newly acquired lifestyle and wound up in the Bowery. He finally got a job packaging and labeling powdered charcoal for eight dollars a week. It was there that he also learned a very valuable lesson – if he wanted to get anywhere in life, it was up to him. He started packaging charcoal as if his life depended on it.

In the meantime, Joseph Binney was busy with his own pursuits. By 1880, he had opened a sales office for his lampblack in New York. Now back on his feet, Harold asked his uncle to give him a try at selling lampblack. By day, he peddled his powdered charcoal; at night, he sold lampblack for his uncle. He was so successful that he soon began selling lampblack full time and his uncle took him into the firm as a partner.

It was at this time that Joseph's son, Edwin Binney, finished school and joined the firm, which was still known as the Peekskill Chemical Works. Edwin traveled, gaining experience as a salesman and making friendships that would prove invaluable in the years to come. In the meantime, Harold traveled back to England on the first of many European business trips. It was in Newcastle, England, that Harold was able to secure the American rights for a new line of red oxide of iron. Back home, Edwin was fascinated with the color possibilities of the oxides. It was through Edwin's quiet persistence that barns all over America were soon being painted with red paint made from the oxides produced at the Peekskill plant.

Binney realized that the company could perform a service to other industries through its knowledge and correct application of pigments and related chemical compounds. He instructed his salesmen to determine the needs of their customers in the field so that the laboratory specialists could look for new ways to fulfill these needs.

# Binney & Smith – The Early Years

In 1903, Edwin Binney (left) and his cousin, C. Harold Smith (right), formed the partnership that is responsible for producing the first box of eight Crayola® Crayons. Today their company, Binney & Smith, makes about three billion Crayola® Crayons annually! *Photograph courtesy of Binney & Smith.*

In 1885, Joseph Binney retired, and cousins C. Harold Smith and Edwin Binney continued their partnership under the firm's new name of Binney & Smith. Although the two were as different as "night and day," their individual strengths and abilities complemented one another, resulting in tremendous growth for the organization. Binney's expertise in the area of finance left Smith free to develop new products and new markets for the Binney & Smith Company. However, it was still a few years before the Crayola® Crayon would make its debut.

In the late 1800s, the company of Binney & Smith revolutionized a new method for making carbon black with natural gas. The black carbon was soon being used in printing inks, paints, rubber boots, stove and shoe polish, typewriter ribbons and other products. At the 1900 Paris Exposition, the carbon blacks made by Binney & Smith received a Gold Medal, the first of many such awards received by the company.

The Peekskill Chemical Company was also instrumental in changing the look of America's highways. The first automobile tires were actually white because of the zinc oxide used in the rubber compound. One enterprising tire manufacturer decided to distinguish its tires from those being made by other companies by tinting its tires silver gray. While experimenting with different compounds, the chemists at Peekskill found that darker tires not only looked different, but also were four to five times more durable than other tires. By 1912, carbon black produced by Binney & Smith was being used by tire manufacturers, such as Goodyear, which found that the carbon added to the wear and safety of their tires.

Cartoon from *The Story of a Rainbow. Photograph courtesy of Binney & Smith.*

The Easton Plant. *Photograph courtesy of Binney & Smith.*

Around 1900, while on a train trip, Edwin Binney met a man named John Ketchum, who owned a talc mine in North Carolina. Ketchum was looking for a location with cheap waterpower where he could grind his talc for commercial use. Edwin knew of the perfect place for the project – an unused piece of property in Easton, Pennsylvania, beside the swift-running Bushkill Creek. An old mill, which was already located there, could be used for grinding the talc. Edwin hired Ketchum to supply the talc, and the Easton plant of Binney & Smith was in business.

Edwin Binney had plans for the talc being made at the new plant. He knew of an old slate quarry ten miles up the creek, where tons of waste slate lay unused. Using this slate combined with cement and Ketchum's talc, the company of Binney & Smith was soon in the slate pencil business. Shortly thereafter, the company began making chalk at the Easton plant.

In 1902, after experimenting with various recipes, Binney & Smith developed their famous An-Du-Septic® white dustless blackboard crayon. This schoolhouse chalk was awarded the Gold Medal at the St. Louis Exposition that year. The chalk enabled students and teachers to do their work better and more easily without endangering their health and without being covered with chalk dust at the end of the school day.

Representatives from the company were sent to schools all over the country to demonstrate the benefits of this new dustless chalk. Traveling from place to place, they reported over and over again that the colored crayons being used by schoolchildren needed to be improved. Although they looked pretty, not much color came off of the crayons and onto the paper. Children needed an inexpensive crayon that worked!

By this time, Binney & Smith had begun looking for a substitute for the messy black inks that were being used for marking crates and barrels for commercial use. They discovered that by combining carbon black with different waxes, they could make thick black wax crayons – Staonal® brand marking crayons – which worked well on paper and wood. Was it possible that the same process could be used to produce quality colored wax crayons at a price that schoolchildren could afford?

Because of his own love of color, along with the fact that his wife had once been a teacher herself, Edwin Binney was particularly fond of the crayon end of the business. He went to work developing a good quality colored crayon that would be inexpensive enough for all schoolchildren to afford. Company researchers soon developed a technique to produce crayons in a variety of colors. However, the pigments being used at the time

A tin of the
An·Du·Septic®
Dustless
Crayons.

were toxic and not suitable for crayons that might be chewed or ingested by children. Pigments were soon developed to replace the organic colors with synthetic non-toxic pigments.

Another challenge involved the actual production of the brightly colored non-toxic crayons. Chemists had to carefully measure and hand-mix small batches of liquid paraffin wax to match the colors uniformly and consistently. Specially trained workers pulled the slim cylinders from their molds. Labels had to be rolled by hand. Although the process was painstaking and time-consuming, it soon paid off. The crayons became an overnight success with children and teachers.

No. 1 Staonal® Marking Crayons.

Molded crayons
and labels from the
Crayola® Factory.

## Chapter 2

# 1903 to 2003:
# A Century of Crayola® Crayons

In 1903, Crayola® made its debut. Edwin's wife, Alice Stead Binney, came up with the name *Crayola*® by combining the French word for chalk, *craie*, with the first part of oleaginous, the oily paraffin wax used to make the crayon. The first box of Crayola® Crayons, which sold for only five cents, included eight colors – Black, Brown, Blue, Red, Violet, Orange, Yellow and Green.

By 1920, Binney & Smith had developed a complete line of colorful products for schoolchildren, as well as for artists. Rubens Crayola®, named for the great artist Peter Paul Rubens, was the company's top quality crayon.

Prior to 1978, Binney & Smith used the brand name Crayola® only on its molded crayons. The company also made crayons such as Perma fine arts crayons, which were the company's pressed (or extruded) standard size crayons. Available in a variety of boxes and tins, they were a popular choice for school use. These crayons, which could be easily sharpened to a fine point, were made using a special manufacturing process that made them strong, as well as colorful. Perma Pressed Crayons were available in a variety of colors and used during the 1920s through the 1970s.

Crayolet and Besco crayons, the brands of choice for school art instruction, were introduced in the 1940s. "Besco" was the name given to the kindergarten size crayons made by Binney & Smith. These regular and Anti·Roll® crayons were available in boxes of eight and sixteen.

Left: A box of the 1903 Crayola® Crayons which originally sold for five cents.

Below: A box of Rubens Crayola® Drawing Crayons, the company's top quality crayon. The back of the box reads: "The only Crayon which Artists consider a substitute for Oil and Water Color and Pastels. Will not blur. Will not wash nor rub off. Studies made with it can be Varnished. Unequalled for outdoor Sketching. CLEAN – COMPACT – CONVENIENT."

Two boxes of Perma Pressed crayons, No. 93 in back and No. 81, open and in the foreground.

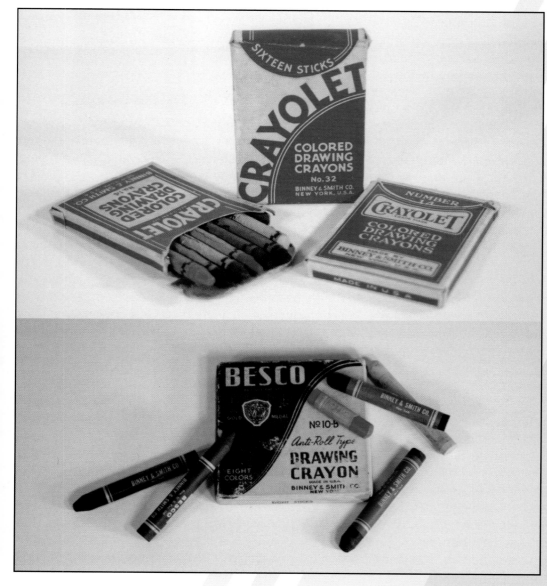

Left: Crayolet and Besco drawing crayons. The Crayolet box standing up in the back contains 16 sticks and is No. 32. The two in the foreground are No. 14. The No. 10-B Besco box contains eight Anti-Roll® drawing crayons.

Left: Two Artista® Water Colors tin containers.

Below: A box of Clayola® Clay. *Photograph courtesy of Sharon Sanford.*

The company also made Artista® oil pastels, water colors and tempera poster paints.

During the Great Depression of the 1930s, Binney & Smith hired local families to hand wrap and label their crayons. Each farm became associated with a particular crayon color. This tradition continued and helped farmers supplement their incomes during the winter months until 1943.

In 1933, Binney & Smith introduced a new product, Clayola® Clay for modeling and sculpting. It was also at this time that the company made a commitment to promote product safety in the art material industry. In 1936, Binney & Smith became a founding member of the Crayon, Water Color and Craft Institute.

During the early years of the Crayola® brand, chalk and crayons had been manufactured and packaged in collectible metal tins and boxes; however, with the onset of World War II and the shortage of metal, these tins began disappearing in the mid-1940s. Today, these are some of the most desirable and valuable "finds" for fervent Crayola® collectors.

It was also around this time that the company initiated a national teacher workshop program to offer in-school training for art teachers about the many ways to use the growing number of Crayola® products. To this day, the support for quality art education and professional development for teachers has always been a priority for the Binney & Smith Company.

In 1949, a new Crayola® box was released that included forty-eight crayons and introduced new colors such as Periwinkle, Prussian Blue and Burnt Sienna. Nine years later, in 1958, the 64-crayon box of Crayola® Crayons made its debut. In this version, which had a built-in crayon sharpener, "Prussian Blue" was renamed "Midnight Blue." This change was made after teachers noted that students were no longer familiar with Prussian history. The follow-

ing year, the first Crayola® advertisements appeared on the popular children's television show, "Ding Dong School" hosted by Miss Frances.

Other additions and changes continued to occur through the years. The color "Flesh" was changed to "Peach" in 1962, and "Indian Red" became "Chestnut" in 1999, recognizing that not everyone's skin color is the same. In the early 1990s, thirty years after changing "Flesh" to "Peach," Binney & Smith became the industry's leader in developing art products such as multicultural crayons, markers and paints that reflected a variety of skin tones. This emphasis on cultural diversity enabled children of all colors to develop a positive respect for themselves and others.

The 1970s brought about a number of changes for the Binney & Smith Company. In 1972, eight new fluorescent colors were released. Four years later, the company relocated its headquarters to Easton, Pennsylvania, having outgrown three different locations in New York City.

In 1977, Binney & Smith bought Silly Putty® – a favorite toy of "kids" from around the world. The synthetic rubber, which was used for a variety of purposes during World War II, was first introduced as a "toy" at the 1950 International Toy Fair. Today, the company produces more than 300 pounds of Silly Putty® each day. The first Crayola® markers were released in 1978 and included the same eight colors featured in the original box of Crayola® Crayons.

In 1984, Binney & Smith became a subsidiary of Hallmarks Cards and introduced the Crayola® Dream-Makers® program. This program was designed to foster art education in elementary schools and recognize children for their artistic endeavors.

Eight Crayola® colors were retired and enshrined in the newly established Crayola® Hall of Fame in 1990. To commemorate the 90th anniversary of Crayola® in 1993, sixteen new colors were introduced and included in the biggest assortment of crayons yet – the Crayola® 96 Big Box. The names for these new colors were selected from over two million suggestions.

In 1996 – ninety-three years after Binney & Smith made the first crayon – the one hundred billionth Crayola® Blue Ribbon Crayon rolled off the production line. Fred Rogers, the host of television's "Mister Rogers' Neighborhood," was given the honor of making the crayon on this historic occasion.

Today Binney & Smith employs more than 1,750 employees and packages products in a dozen different languages. The company produces an average of eleven million crayons a day – approximately three billion each year.

The formula for Crayola® Crayons, which is essentially the same one used in 1903, is as guarded today as it was then. Outside of the crayon production area, heated tanks store liquid paraffin wax. This heated wax is pumped directly into a mixing vat and mixed with a carefully measured amount of powdered pigment. The wax is then poured from a double-spouted bucket onto the molding table. Each mold forms 2,400 crayons.

As the wax pigment blend settles into the cylindrical mold, it is cooled by water. The nature of each color's pigments also determines how long the crayon will take to cool – from four to seven minutes.

At this point, the crayons are hydraulically ejected from their molds. The first quality control check is made as the mold operator empties the crayons from their rack onto a worktable. Any crayons with broken tips, chipped ends or inconsistent colors are returned to the mixing vat to be melted and remolded. Of course, automated labeling machines now wrap and glue

A Crayola® Big Box. Certified "Non-Toxic," this box has a built-in sharpener and contains 96 crayons.

A Crayola® Crayons Color Drawing Set with 72 crayons, from 1968. It also came with a project book, a drawing book, a sharpener (which can be seen in the upper left-hand corner of the box) and crayon trays.

on the labels, a process which is quite a bit faster than the hand labeling method that was used in the early and mid-1900s. After crayons are labeled, they are fed into packing machines that collate the colors into different assortments.

For their first hundred years, Crayola® Crayons have had an interesting and colorful history. The future looks bright for those of us who continue to enjoy these treasured memories from our childhood.

Clockwise:
Crayola® crayons are made from two basic ingredients: paraffin wax and colored pigment. The wax blend is delivered to Binney & Smith in heated train cars and stored in two-story silos.

The wax blend is pumped into the factory, where it is mixed with pigment in large, heated kettles. Once mixed, the blend is poured into special two-spouted buckets.

The mixture is then poured into crayon-shaped molds. As the mixture cools, the crayons solidify.

Clockwise:
Cooled crayons are ejected from the molds.

Crayola® crayons are hand-inspected for quality. Crayons with imperfections are re-melted.

Each crayon gets a double-wrapped label with the distinctive Crayola® logo and trademark - and, of course, the color name!

# Part II: The ABC's Crayola® Collectibles

This section features photographs of items in the categories listed below. Descriptions and pricing information for these and other collectibles may be found in Part IV: A Collector's Guide to Crayola® Collectibles.

## Chapter 3

# Advertisements

Clockwise:
An advertisement from 1918 for a "Crayola®" drawing contest.

Binney & Smith calendar blotters from December 1926 and November 1927.

A Crayola® advertisement from December 1927.

An assortment of Crayola® advertisements shown with the products.

Advertisement in *The Drawing Teacher*, from the 1930s, with the box of advertised crayons.

Advertisement for "50 years of Crayola® Leadership," in *The Art Educationist*, from January – February 1953.

Top: A Crayola® elf blotter, circa. 1950.

Middle: A "50 Years of Crayola® Leadership" blotter from 1953.

Left: A Crayola® box display sign, circa 1958.

Awakening to the wonderful world of color ...remember?

Inspire the secret dreams and bold accomplishments
that only children know. Give them the means to
explore and relight your own glad memories. Act soon
...before the dreams of youth escape, beyond recapture.

Clockwise:
A Crayola® advertisement from 1957.

A Crayola® advertisement, circa 1962.

A Crayola® advertisement, circa 1965.

Left: Top to Bottom:
Free Crayola® Crayons from Double Cola, circa 1970.

McDonald's CosMc Crayola® Happy Meal and crayons from 1987.

Advertisement from the Crayola® advertising campaign from 2000.

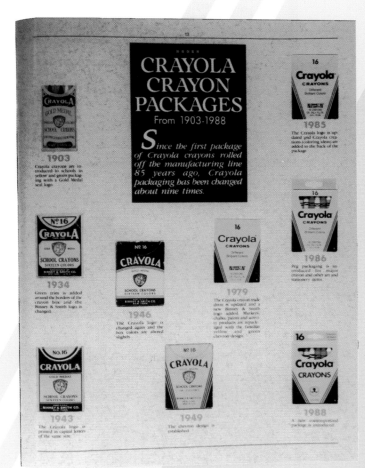

Crayola® Crayon packages from 1903 to 1988, from Binney & Smith *Rainbow Reporter*.

## Chapter 4

# Art

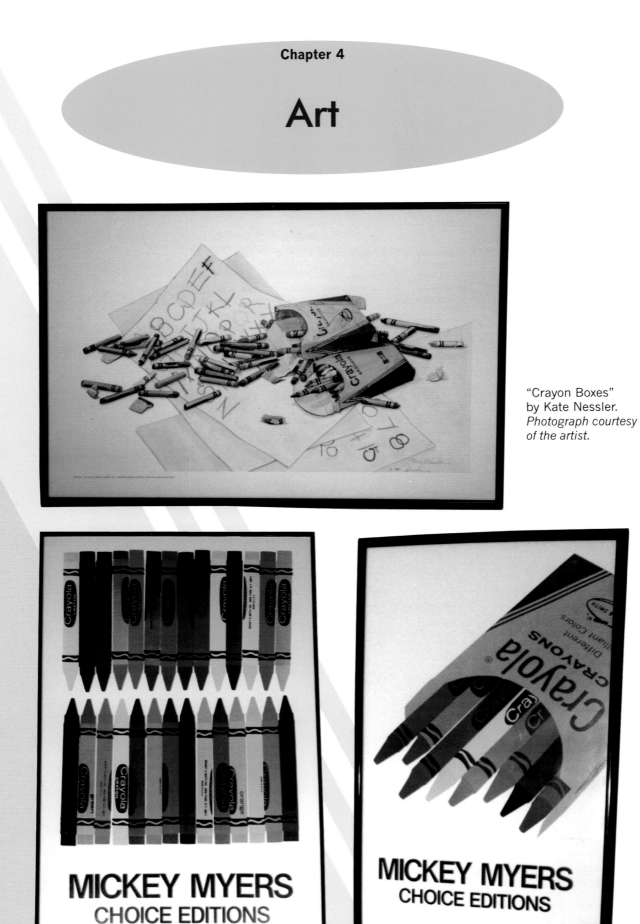

"Crayon Boxes"
by Kate Nessler.
*Photograph courtesy
of the artist.*

**MICKEY MYERS**
CHOICE EDITIONS

**MICKEY MYERS**
CHOICE EDITIONS

"Mickey Myers Choice Editions" poster from
1979. *Photograph courtesy of the artist.*

"Mickey Myers Choice Editions" poster from
1979. *Photograph courtesy of the artist.*

"Uncle Sam with Crayola® Crayons," circa 1987, from the Smithsonian Archives Binney & Smith Collection. *Photograph used with permission of Binney & Smith.*

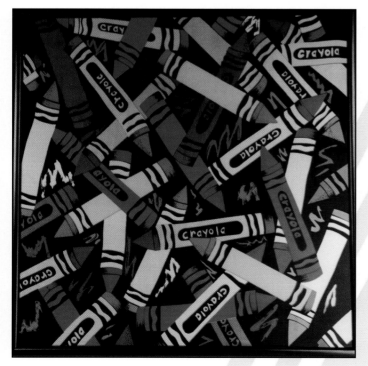

A framed Crayola® Crayon scarf from the 1990s.

"The Vision" by Ron DeLong, from 1998. The artist was commissioned by Binney & Smith to sculpt this piece for the company. *Photograph used with permission of Binney & Smith.*

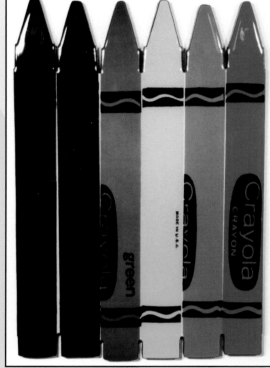

Above: A photograph – "Color Spills" by Gail Farrell, circa 1995. *Courtesy of the photographer.*

Left: "Six Crayola® Crayons," an acrylic wall hanging, from Mickey Myers Expo, Gallery 92, 1991.

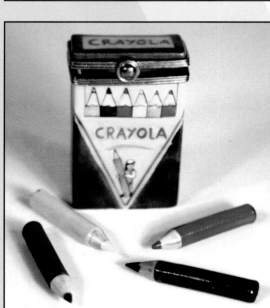

Above: "Crayola® Crayons" by Tony Azzito. *Photograph courtesy of Janet Swahn, ART4SALE.*

Left: A Limoges Crayola box with crayons, from 1999.

## Chapter 5

# Books and Other Publications

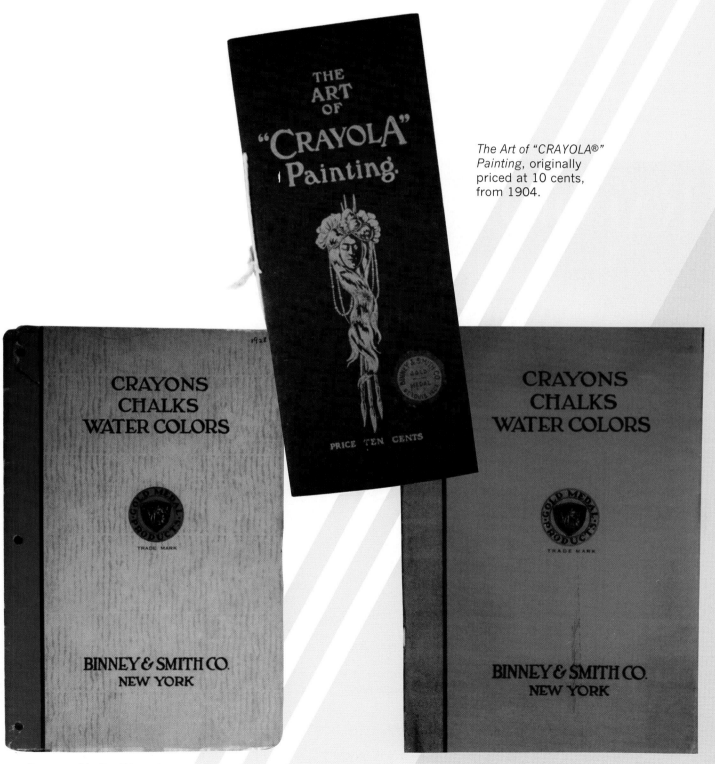

*The Art of "CRAYOLA®" Painting*, originally priced at 10 cents, from 1904.

*Crayons, Chalks, Water Colors* from 1928.

*Crayons, Chalks, Water Colors* from 1930.

*The Drawing Teacher* containing teaching projects for art teachers, from 1937 and 1939.

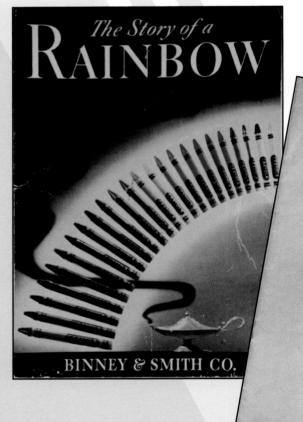

Left to Right:
*The Story of a Rainbow*, a company booklet prepared for the employees of Binney & Smith in 1947. While it gives important historical information about the company, it was apparently printed to explain benefits to new employees joining the company after World War II.

*The B & S Rainbow Reporter*, for April – September 1953.

*The Art Educationist*, from May – June 1953.

Gold Medal Products for Art Education, circa 1953 to 1954.

*Artista® Water Colors*, from 1954.

Above: The English version of *Learning to Use Your Crayola® Crayons*, from 1976.

Right: The Spanish version of *Learning to Use Your Crayola® Crayons*, titled *Aprendiendo a usar crayons Crayola®*, from circa 1976.

**Crayola Crayons Art Techniques**

*Crayola® Crayons Art Techniques*, from 1991.

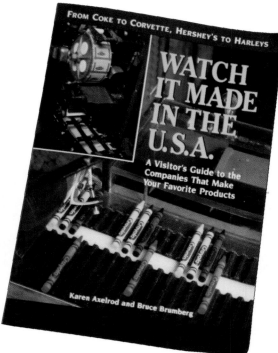

*Watch It Made In the USA*, from 2001.

*The Rainbow Reporter*, from Summer 1988.

*The Rainbow Reporter*, from Winter 1993.

# Children's Books

Two *Color 'n' Draw Fold-A-Books*, one with the alphabet, the other with a train circus parade, from 1977. These books featured Easy-Off crayons for coloring and re-coloring.

A *Crayola® Fold-A-Book*, a color and re-color storybook entitled *Beautiful Seasons*, from 1980. Eight Easy-Off Crayola® crayons were included.

*How is a Crayon Made?* by Oz Charles, from 1988 and *Crayons From Start to Finish* by Samuel G. Woods, from 1999.

A Crayola® pop-up book entitled *Crayola® Bunny Saves the Day*, from 1990.

## Chapter 6

# Chalk, Pastels and Pencils

Early An·Du·Septic® Slate Pencils. The box states that they are "hygienic and guaranteed free from grit." *Photograph courtesy of Sharon Sanford.*

A box of seven sticks of UVA (Uniform Value Assured) Assorted Chalk Crayons, No. 702, circa 1924. *Photograph courtesy of Sharon Sanford.*

Three vintage wooden chalk boxes. The top one held Atlantic White Chalk Crayons No. 307; the middle one contained An·Du·Septic® Sight Saver Crayons; and the bottom one held Yellow Enamel Best School Crayons.

Far Left: A box of three sticks of UVA (Uniform Value Assured) Little Folks Chalk Crayons, No. 3043, circa 1927.

A box of three sticks of UVA (Uniform Value Assured) Little Folks Chalk Crayons, No. 7023, circa 1927.

A box of eight "Spectra" Pastel Crayons, circa 1927.

Far Right: A box of eight Spectra Pastel Crayons, No. 15, circa 1927 to 1930.

A box of eight "Spectra" Pastel Crayons, No. 21, circa 1927 to 1930.

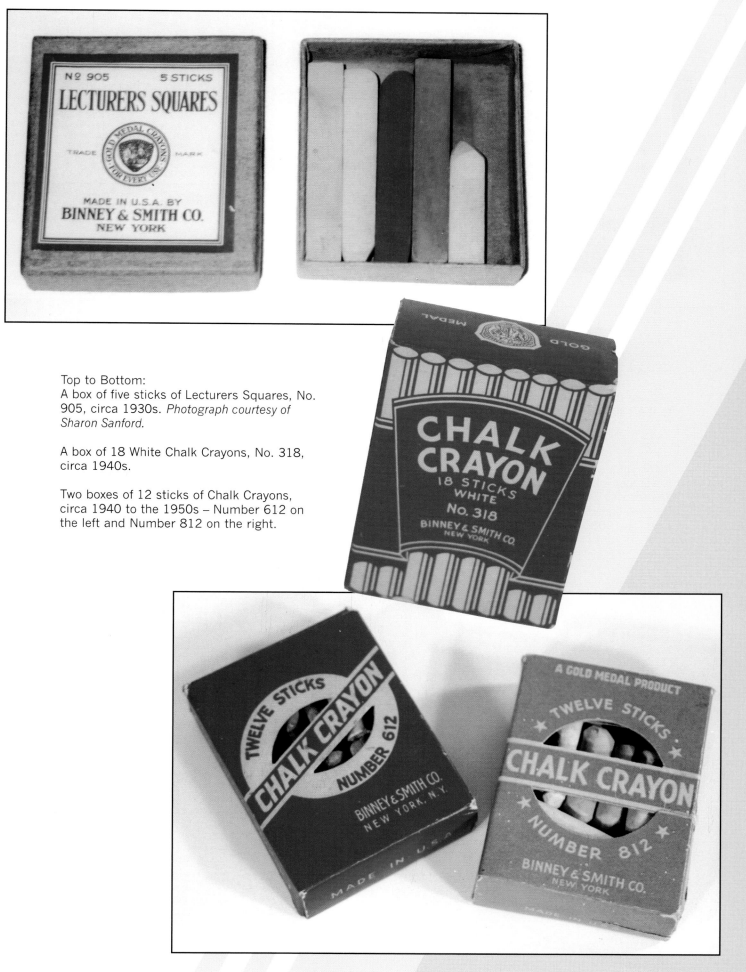

Top to Bottom:
A box of five sticks of Lecturers Squares, No. 905, circa 1930s. *Photograph courtesy of Sharon Sanford.*

A box of 18 White Chalk Crayons, No. 318, circa 1940s.

Two boxes of 12 sticks of Chalk Crayons, circa 1940 to the 1950s – Number 612 on the left and Number 812 on the right.

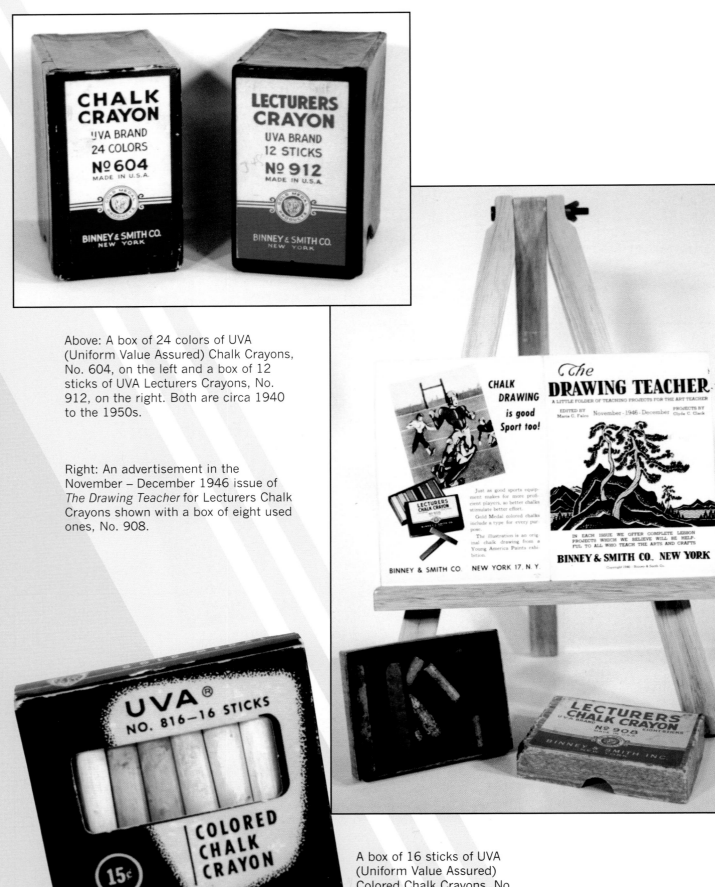

Above: A box of 24 colors of UVA (Uniform Value Assured) Chalk Crayons, No. 604, on the left and a box of 12 sticks of UVA Lecturers Crayons, No. 912, on the right. Both are circa 1940 to the 1950s.

Right: An advertisement in the November – December 1946 issue of *The Drawing Teacher* for Lecturers Chalk Crayons shown with a box of eight used ones, No. 908.

A box of 16 sticks of UVA (Uniform Value Assured) Colored Chalk Crayons, No. 816, from 1950 to the 1960s. This box originally sold for 15 cents.

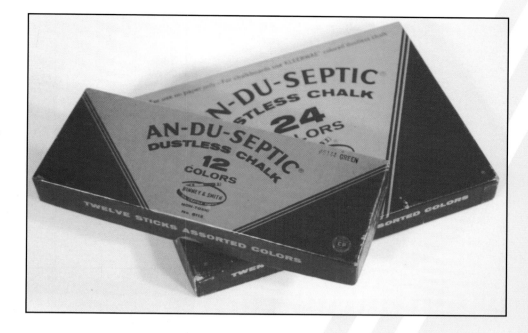

Two boxes of An-Du-Septic® Dustless Chalk, from 1958. No. 6112, on top, has 12 colors while the one on the bottom, No. 5144, has 24 colors.

Left: Three boxes of 16 sticks of No. 816 Colored Chalk Crayon from 1950 to the 1960s. Note the original price of 15 cents on two of the boxes.

A No. 320 box of 20 sticks of White Chalk, circa 1968. The original price was 15 cents.

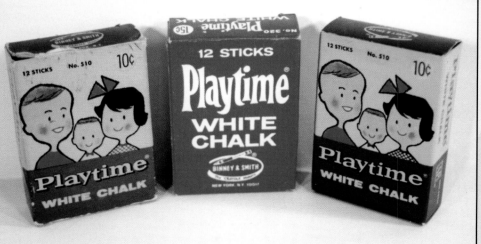

Three boxes of 12 sticks of Playtime White Chalk from 1968 to the 1970s. The middle box is No. 320 and sold for 15 cents. The two with the drawings of children on them are both No. 510 and sold for 10 cents each.

Back view of a box of 12 Batons Craie Blanche Swan Crayons, circa 1970. The box says "Canada Crayon Co. The Crayola® Makers."

Above: A box of 36 sticks of Artista® Colored Poster Chalk, No. 136, from the 1970s, and a box of 12 Arista® Oil Pastels, from 1964 to the 1970s.

Left: A box of 12 sticks of Crayola® An-Du-Septic® Chalk, No. 1400, from the 1980s. The front of the box indicates it is "White Low Dust Chalk, Easy to Erase."

## Chapter 7

# Crayons

## Pressed Crayons

The "Crayola®" name was not used on any product
except for molded crayons until 1978.

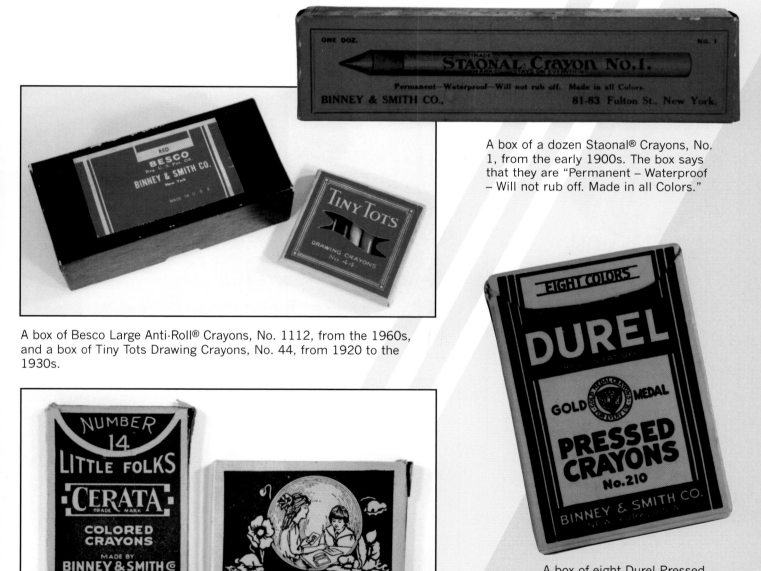

A box of a dozen Staonal® Crayons, No.
1, from the early 1900s. The box says
that they are "Permanent – Waterproof
– Will not rub off. Made in all Colors."

A box of Besco Large Anti-Roll® Crayons, No. 1112, from the 1960s,
and a box of Tiny Tots Drawing Crayons, No. 44, from 1920 to the
1930s.

A box of eight Durel Pressed
Crayons, No. 210, circa 1928.

The front and back of two boxes of Little Folks Cerata Colored Crayons,
Number 14, circa 1927.

Right Top to Bottom:
A box of 22 Munsell Perma Pressed Crayons, No. 220M, from the 1930s.

Four assorted boxes of Perma Pressed Crayon Boxes, No. 85, from the 1940s to the 1950s. Each box contains 16 crayons.

Two boxes of Easy-Off crayons from the 1950s. The box on the left is No. 30 and contains 12 crayons; the one on the right is No. 41 and contains eight crayons.

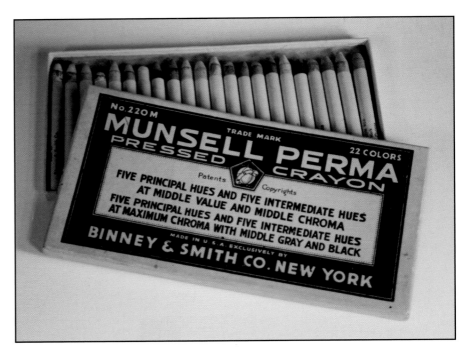

A box of eight Anti-Roll® Drawing Crayons, No. 25, circa 1940s.

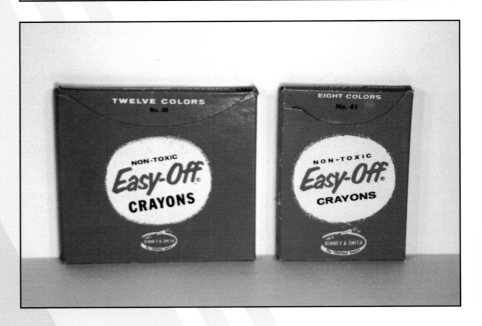

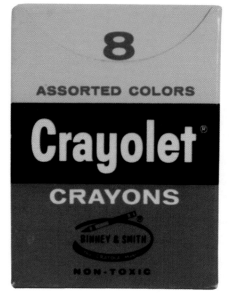

A box of eight Crayolet Crayons, No. 14, circa 1959.

A box of six Crayolet Crayons No. 14, from the 1960s. The original price was five cents.

A box of 12 Besco Large Anti-Roll® Pressed Crayons, in bulk, No. 1112, from 1959. This box contains all one color – Peach.

Above: Two boxes of No. 60 Washable Crayons from 1968. The box on the left contains 24 crayons and originally sold for 29 cents while the one on the right contains only 12 crayons and was priced at 19 cents.

Left: A box of eight large Artista II® Anti-Roll® Crayons, No. 2108, from 1996.

# Molded Crayons

An original box of eight No. 8 "Crayola®" Crayons from 1903.

A collection of vintage Crayola® Crayon boxes shown in *The Art of Crayola® Painting*, from 1904. The boxes appear about one-twelfth their actual size.

No. 1 Black
No. 2 Charcoal Gray
No. 3 White
No. 4 Purple
No. 5 Prussian Blue
No. 6 Celestial Blue
No. 7 Ultramarine Blue
No. 8 Cobalt Blue
No. 9 Chrome Green, Dark
No. 10 Chrome Green, Medium
No. 11 Chrome Green, Light
No. 12 Olive Green
No. 13 Van Dyke Brown
No. 14 Indian Red
No. 15 Raw Umber
No. 16 Burnt Umber
No. 17 Raw Sienna
No. 18 Burnt Sienna
No. 19 Golden Ochre
No. 20 Madder Lake
No. 21 English Vermilion
No. 22 Rose Pink
No. 23 Flesh Tint
No. 24 Venetian Red, Light
No. 25 Venetian Red, Dark
No. 26 Lemon Yellow
No. 27 Medium Yellow
No. 28 Orange

TWENTY-EIGHT
BRIGHT ASSORTED COLORS

The front and back view of a box of 28 "Crayola®" Young Artists Drawing Crayons, No. 51, circa 1904.

A box of No. 57 "Crayola®" Young Artists Drawing Crayons, circa 1904. *Photograph Courtesy of Sharon Sanford.*

An original box of 16 "Crayola®" Crayons, No. 16, circa 1910.

A box of 24 "Rubens" Crayola® Artists' Crayons, No. 24, circa 1913. The box states: "The Colors in these Crayons are equal to those used in the best Artists' Tube Colors and Pastels."

Left: Two boxes of Rubens Crayola® Crayons, circa 1913 to the 1920s. The box on the left is No. 14 and holds 24 crayons. The open box in the foreground is No. 12 and holds 12 crayons.

A page from the Gold Medal Products Sales Catalog showing the various products, circa 1920s.

# GOLD MEDAL PRODUCTS

No. 93

(Metal Boxed)

No. 14

No. 50

No. 8

No. 25

No. 412

No. 75

No. 812

MADE BY BINNEY & SMITH CO., N. Y.

Two boxes of Crayola® Gold Medal School Crayons, from 1913 to the 1920s. No. 16, on the left, contains 16 crayons, while No. 6, open and in the foreground, holds six crayons.

A box of 16 Crayola® School Crayons, No. 16, from the 1930s.

A box of eight Canadian Crayola® School Crayons, No. 8, circa 1933. Note the spelling of "colours" on the package.

A box of eight Crayola® School Crayons, No. 8, from 1947.

Above: Two boxes of Crayola® Drawing Crayons from the 1940s to the 1950s. No. 38, on the left, has eight crayons. No. 24, on the right, has "Rubens Crayola® Crayon" on the package.

Left: A box of 24 Crayola® Drawing Crayons, No. 241, from the 1940s to the 1950s.

Above: Three boxes of eight large and jumbo Crayola® Crayons, No. 38, from the 1940s and 1950s.

Left: A box of Crayola® Gold Medal School Crayons, No. 836, from 1953.

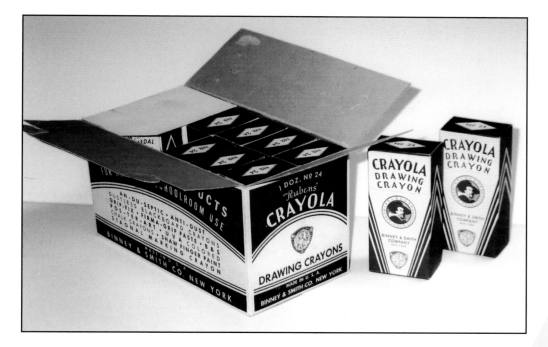

Above: A case containing a dozen boxes of No. 24 Crayola® Drawing Crayons, circa 1953. *Photograph courtesy of Sharon Sanford.*

Right: Two boxes of Crayola® Drawing Crayons, Nos. 48 and 24, from 1953.

Front and back view of a box of 64 Crayola® Crayons, No. 64, with a built-in sharpener, from 1958. The original price for this box was $1.19.

A box of 72 Crayola® Crayons and sharpener, No. 72, with a book of crayon projects titled *Crayola® Crayon Project Book*, from 1959. The sharpener can be seen in the upper right-hand corner of the box.

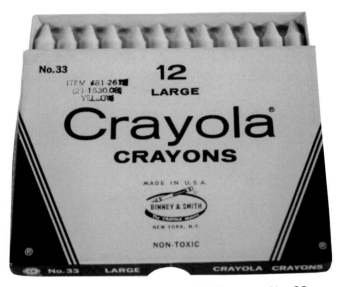

A box of 12 Large Yellow Crayola® Crayons, No. 33, circa 1962.

Above: A cylindrical canister of 48 Crayola® Crayons, No. 480, from the 1960s. The original price of 75 cents was reduced to 59 cents.

Right: A box of eight Crayola® Crayons, No. 8, from 1963. Note that the box indicates they are "Different Brilliant Colors."

Two boxes of Crayola® Crayons. The box of 16 "Different Brilliant Colors," on the left, No. 161, circa 1964, originally sold for 30 cents. The box of 16 "School Crayons," on the right, is No. 16.

A box of 16 Large Crayola® Crayons of "Different Brilliant Colors," No. 336A, circa 1965.

A box of 16 Crayola® Crayons of "Different Brilliant Colors," No. 16-P, in a "NEW plastic container," from 1968.

A box of 24 Crayola® Imagination Station Crayons, made especially for Hallmark, from 1987.

Left: Three boxes of eight, 16 and 24 Crayola® Crayons with the "smile" design on the box, from 1988.

Below: A variety of promotional Crayola® Crayon boxes from the 1980s and 1990s.

Above: A box of eight Crayola® Bunny Pastel Crayons, originally selling for $1.00, and a box of 24 Crayola® Bunny Crayons, originally selling for $2.10. Both are from 1990. *Photograph courtesy of Sharon Sanford.*

Right: A box of eight Crayola® Pastel Crayons, from 1990. The box says "Soft Light Colors."

A box of eight Crayola® Colour 'n Smell Crayons from Canada, circa 1992. There is even a maple leaf on the box.

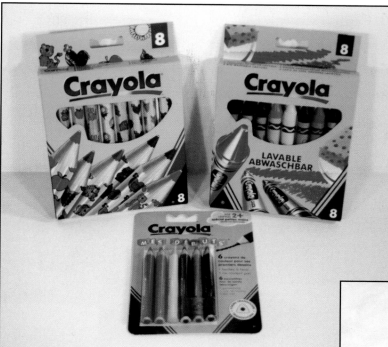

Two boxes of eight Crayola® Crayons and one package of Crayola® Colored Pencils, from 1994 to 2000, all from Europe.

A box of Mickey's Stuff for Kids featuring 16 "no-roll" Crayola® Crayons, No. 21-5299, from 1995. *Photograph courtesy of Sharon Sanford.*

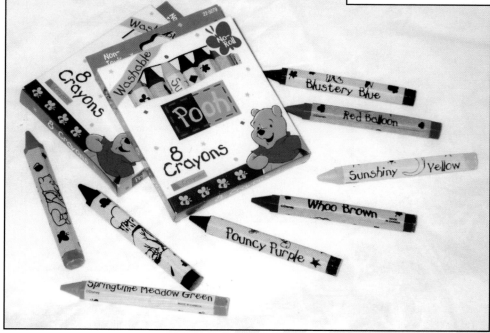

A box of eight Crayola® Flat Tops No-Roll Crayons, from 1995. *Photograph courtesy of Sharon Sanford.*

Two boxes of eight no-roll Crayola® Pooh Washable Crayons, No. 22-5279, from 1995. This set featured color names such as Springtime Meadow Green, Pouncy Purple, Whoo Brown, Sunshiny Yellow, Red Balloon and Blustery Blue. *Photograph courtesy of Sharon Sanford.*

Four assorted boxes of Crayola® Crayons from Canada, circa 1995 to 1998.

A box of 24 Crayola® Crayons from Canada, circa 1998.

Two boxes of eight Crayola® Crayons in "Favorite Colours of Canada," from Canada, circa 1998.

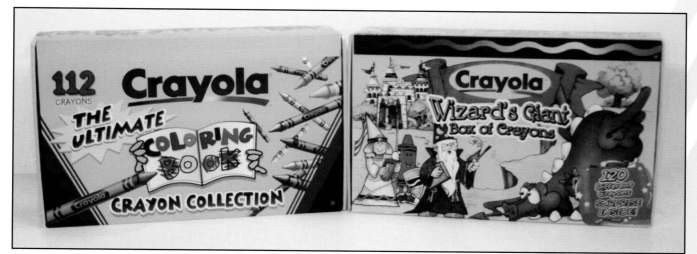

Above: Two large boxes of Crayola® Crayons. The box on the left, from 1997, contains 112 crayons and boasts that it is "The Ultimate Coloring Book Crayon Collection." The box on the right, from 1999, has 120 crayons and is the "Wizard's Giant Box of Crayons."

Left: A Crayola® Metallic Sample Kit which was free with an Energizer purchase, from 2000. The package contains four Crayola® metallic crayons, two metallic markers and a construction paper pad.

Above: Two boxes of 12 Crayola® Crayons – old and new. The box on the left is from 1970 and the box on the right is from 2000.

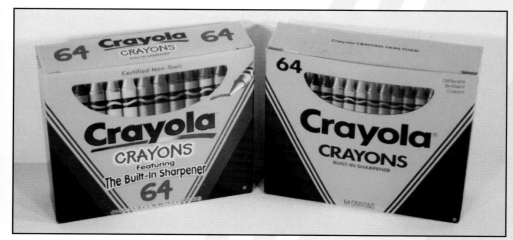

Left: Two boxes of 64 Crayola® Crayons, both with the "smile" design on the box and a built-in sharpener. The box on the left is from 1997 and the one on the right is from 1990.

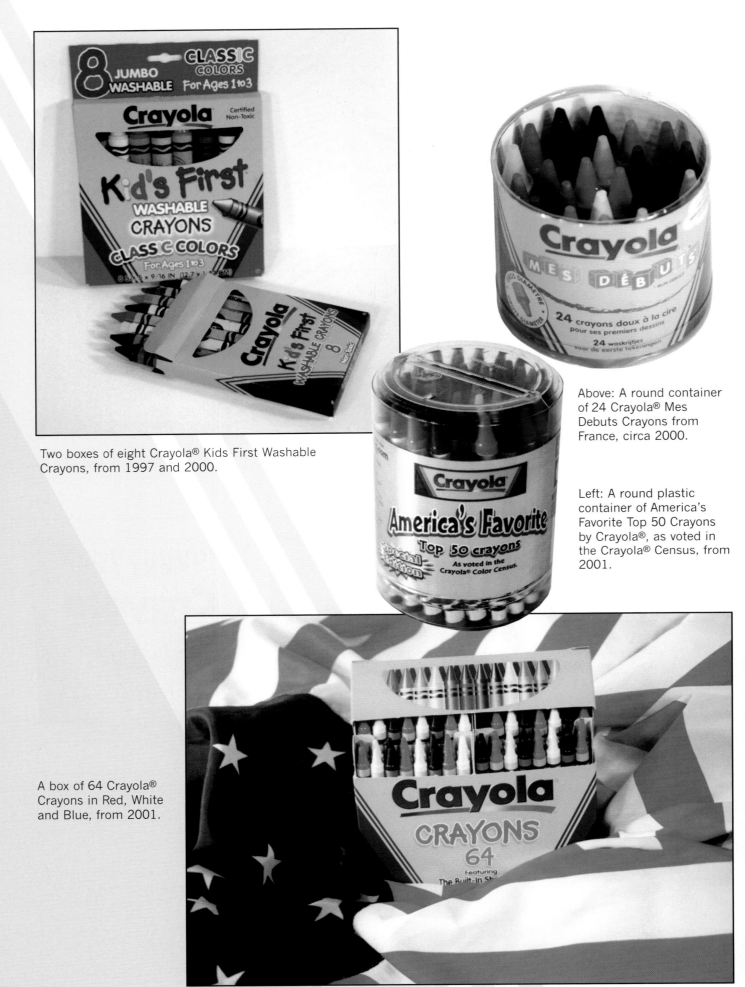

Two boxes of eight Crayola® Kids First Washable Crayons, from 1997 and 2000.

Above: A round container of 24 Crayola® Mes Debuts Crayons from France, circa 2000.

Left: A round plastic container of America's Favorite Top 50 Crayons by Crayola®, as voted in the Crayola® Census, from 2001.

A box of 64 Crayola® Crayons in Red, White and Blue, from 2001.

## Chapter 8

# Dolls, Animals and Plush Toys

Above: Six Crayola® Bears from 1986.

A large Blue Crayola® Bear shown with two medium-sized bears – a Yellow Crayola® Bear and a Green Crayola® Bear, from 1986.

A set of four Burger King Promotional Crayola® Bears, from 1986.

Left: A Pink Crayola® Bunny from 1988.

Below: Crayola® Lavender Lou Bunny in Paint Can from 1989 shown with a Yellow Crayola® Bunny from 1988.

A Blue Crayola® Circus Elephant from 1989.

A Yellow Crayola® Circus Monkey holding a Red Crayola® Dog, from 1989.

Right: A Purple Crayola® Circus Horse from 1989. *Photograph courtesy of Sharon Sanford.*

Below: A Green Crayola® Circus Lion from 1989.

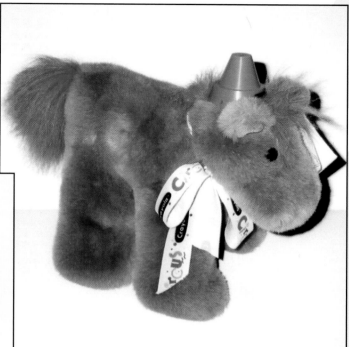

Above: Yellow Crayola® Daffadilly Duck and Squiggles, from 1990.

Left: Pink Crayola® Painter Candy Cotton Tail and White Painter Bunny, from 1990.

Left: Blue Crayola® Boy and Pink Crayola® Girl, circa 1990.

Below: Green Crayola® Football Player and Hot Pink Crayola® Cheerleader, from 1991.

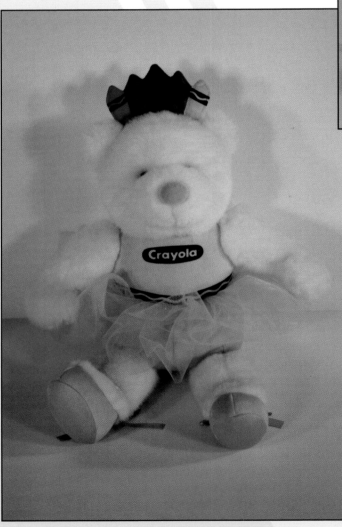

White Crayola® Ballerina Bear in her pink tutu, circa 1996.

Light brown Crayola® Bear wearing a red Crayola® shirt and a multicolored beanie, circa 1996.

Right: Light brown Crayola® Bear in a Crayola®
Rainbow Sweater, circa 1996.

Below: Crayola® Storybook Friends Bonnie and
Lonnie, from 1997.

Above: Four 8-inch Madame Alexander Dolls, left
to right: *Crayola® Green, Crayola® Red, Crayola®
Yellow* and *Crayola® Blue*, from 1999.

Left: Madame Alexander's 14-inch *Crayola® Megan*
from 1999.

Crayola® "Tip" Plush Key Chains in red, yellow and blue, from 1999.

Crayola® Kangaroo from 2000.

Right: Mary Kay Honey Bee Bear and Crayola® Set from 2000.

## Chapter 9

# Lunchboxes, Pencil Boxes and Other Containers

Crayola® CLAY TIME container, featuring Jim Henson's Muppets, from 1982.

THE Crayola® BOX, No. 1010, a vinyl storage box containing 16 crayons, two markers, eight fluorescent crayons, 12 colorful chalk sticks and one crayon sharpener, from 1982.

An undated rustic wooden box of unknown origin with "Crayola" on the top.

An undated glass canister of unknown origin with "Crayola" etched on the side.

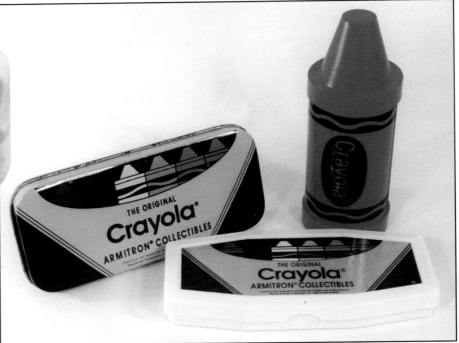

Plastic and Tin Crayola® Watch Containers from 1984 to the 1990s.

A yellow Crayola® Crayon Bank, circa 1987.

Right: Purple and clear Crayola® Crayon Bank, circa 1980 to the 1990s.

Crayola® So Big® Bucket from 1989.

Red and blue Crayola® Crayon
Pencil Boxes with Crayola®
Crayon Box design, circa
1990s.

Blue and red Crayola® Crayon
Pencil Boxes with children's
drawings designs, circa 1990s.

Above: A plastic Crayola® Lunchbox and
Thermos from 1991.

Left: A vinyl Crayola® Lunchbox and Thermos
from 1991.

Clockwise:
A Crayola® Gold Medal Colors Pencil Box from 1993.

Crayola® Crayon-shaped Cheerios Box container from 1994.

Crayola® Crayon Pencil Box with Calculator, circa 1990s.

Crayola® Time Capsule, circa 2000.

Crayola® Creative Gardens Planter and plant identification stake, circa 2001.

Canadian Crayola® "Tip" the Colour Keeper, circa. 2001.

Crayola® Lots-a-Paint Bucket containing seven bottles of Crayola® Washable Kid's Paint, 16-Pan Crayola® Washable Water Color Paints, two paint brushes, painting sponges, an art smock, project cards and paper, from 2001.

67

## Chapter 10

# Memorabilia and Collectibles

## Crayola® Color and Paint Sets, Toy Sets and Games

A page from *Crayons, Chalks, Water Colors* showing Crayola® Color and Paint Sets from 1928 to 1930.

Another page from *Crayons, Chalks, Water Colors* showing Crayola® Color and Paint Sets from 1928 to 1930.

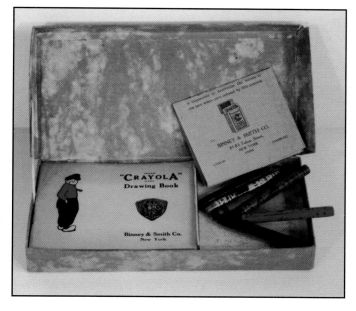

A "Crayola®" Little Folks Outfit, No. 25, from the 1920s. The set included 12 assorted Crayola® Crayons, stencils and a drawing book and paper.

A "Crayola®" Little Folks Outfit, No. 50, from the 1920s. The set included 12 assorted Crayola® Crayons, stencils and a drawing book and paper.

A Crayola® Color Wheel Game from 1981.

A Crayola® Creative Lettering Kit from 1989.

Crayola® Colorable Playing Cards with a box of four Crayola® Crayons, from 1997.

# Binney & Smith Memorabilia

An authentic Crayola®
Factory Stock Box
with a *Certificate of
Authenticity* stating
it was used from
1903 to 1996.

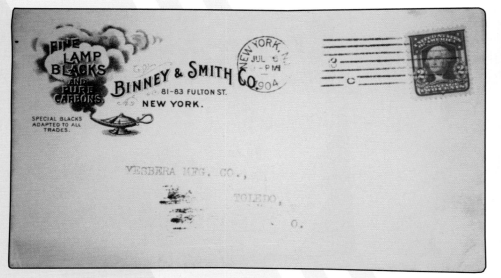

A Binney & Smith company envelope postmarked July 5, 1904.

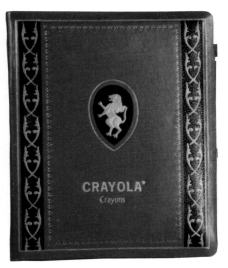

A Crayola® Crayons Notebook,
used by a Binney & Smith sales
employee, circa 1950 to the
1960s.

A Crayola® Crayons Store Display Rack, circa 1958.

The front view of the Binney & Smith "Defend America Coin Saving Book," distributed by the company to schoolchildren. It dates from the 1940s.

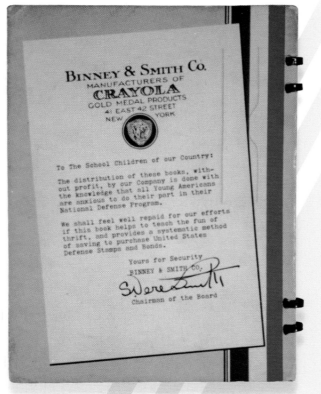

The back view of the "Defend America Coin Saving Book" with a letter from Binney & Smith explaining the purpose of the book.

The inside view of two pages from the "Defend America Coin Saving Book."

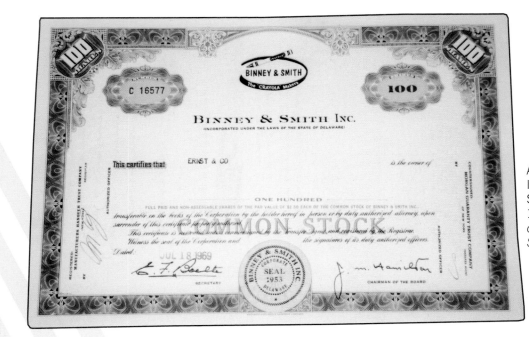

A Binney & Smith, Inc., Common Stock Bond from 1969. *Photograph courtesy of Sharon Sanford.*

A Crayola® Box 75th Anniversary Paperweight from 1977.

A Crayola® Box 90th Anniversary Paperweight from 1993.

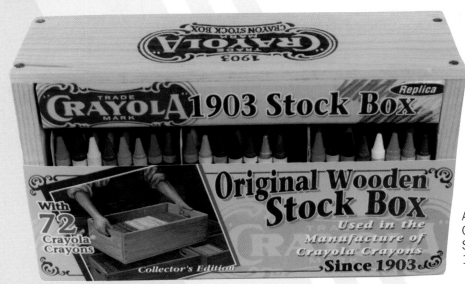

A replica of original Crayola® 1903 Stock Box from 1997.

# Other Crayola® Collectibles

A Dept. 56 North Pole *Crayola® Polar Palette Art Center* and *Crayola® Cruisin' Elves*, from 2000.

Above: A "Happy Holidays from Binney & Smith" Commemorative Plate from 2001.

Left: "Colorful Days Are Spent With You," a limited edition Cherished Teddies Figurine featuring "Rosemary" and her Crayola® Crayons, from 2001.

## Chapter 11

# Novelty Items

Above: Crayola® Men's Handkerchiefs from 1981.

Left: A Crayola® Crayons Record Player from 1981.

Two Crayola® Plastic Plates from 1984.

An undated McCoy Cookie Jar often referred to as the "Crayola Kid Cookie Jar" because of the crayon drawing of a little boy. It is undated. This is one of three Crayola Kid Cookie Jars made by McCoy.

A set of four Crayola® Crayon Box Glasses, circa 1980s.

A Crayola® Novelty Pillow, circa 1980s.

Above Left: Original Drawing Design for a Crayola® Tie, circa 1981, from the Smithsonian Archives Binney & Smith Collection. *Photograph used with permission of Binney & Smith.*

Above Right: Look Closely! Can You Spot the Fake Crayola® Crayon Tie? (The one on the left!) The ties are circa 1982 to the 1990s.

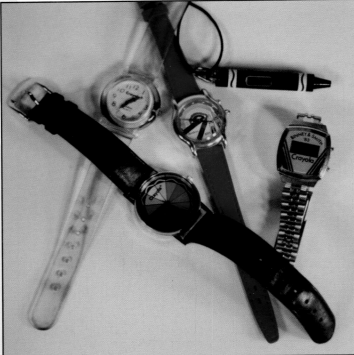

Left: An assortment of Crayola® Watches from 1984 to the 1990s.

Below: A Crayola® Wall Clock, circa 1984 to the 1990s.

Crayola® Box Lip Gloss by Avon, circa 1990s.

Left: A Crayola® Aquarium from 1990.

Right: A Crayola® License Plate, from the 1990s, with Crayola® Easel by Hallmark, from 1999.

A Crayola® Wind-up Clock, from 1991, with a Cube Crayola® Snooze Clock and AM/FM Radio, from 1999.

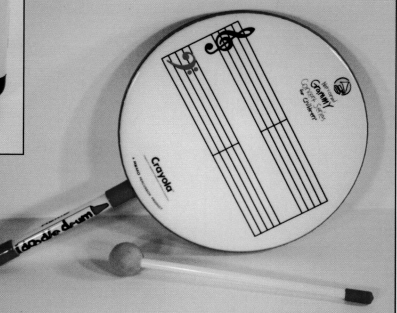

A rare Crayola® Drum and Mallet Set, circa 1990s.

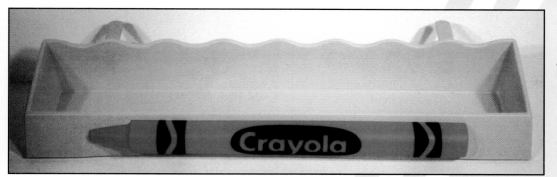

A Crayola® Plastic Display Tray from 1992.

Three Crayola® Night Lights from 1993.

Crayola® Rocks,
an AM/FM Radio
from 1994.

A Crayola® Bathroom Set
of a toothbrush holder and
soap dish, circa 1993.

A Crayola® Mailbox Bank, circa 1998.

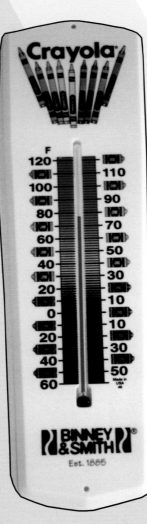

Left: A Crayola® Room Thermometer,
circa 1999.

Right: A Crayola® Table and Chair Set
by Hallmark, from 1999, with a
three-dimensional giant Crayola®
Advertising Box, circa 1993.

## Chapter 12

# Ornaments and Miniatures

## Holiday Collection

A miniature Christmas tree decorated with Hallmark Crayola® Collectible Ornaments.

*Bright Christmas Dreams*, a Hallmark Crayola® ornament from 1987.

*Teacher*, a Hallmark Crayola® ornament from 1988.

*Bright Journey*, a Hallmark Crayola® ornament from 1989.

*Bright Moving Colors*, a Hallmark Crayola® ornament from 1990.

*Bright Vibrant Carols*, a Hallmark Crayola® ornament from 1991.

*Bright Blazing Colors*, a Hallmark Crayola® ornament from 1992.

Bright Shining Castle, a
Hallmark Crayola®
ornament from 1993.

Bright Playful Colors, a
Hallmark Crayola®
ornament from 1994.

Colorful World, a Hallmark Crayola® ornament
from 1995.

Bright 'n' Sunny Tepee, a Hallmark Crayola® ornament
from 1995.

*Bright Flying Colors*, a Hallmark Crayola® ornament from 1996.

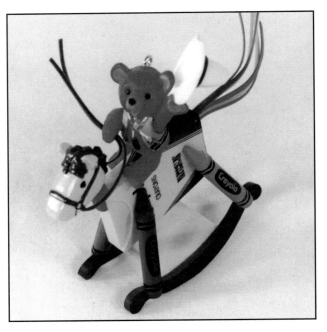

*Bright Rocking Colors*, a Hallmark Crayola® ornament from 1997.

*Bright Sledding Colors*, a Hallmark Crayola® ornament from 1998.

*Clownin' Around*, a Hallmark Crayola® ornament from 1999.

*King of the Ring*, a Hallmark Crayola® ornament from 2000.

Front and back views of the *Crayola® Backpack Bear*, a Hallmark Crayola® ornament from 2000.

Below: Bear with Drum, a Hallmark Crayola® ornament from 1992. It came as a holiday pack with a box of 24 crayons.

Above: *Crayola® Crew Chief*, a Hallmark Crayola® ornament from 2001.

Right: Felt Crayola® Bear, a Hallmark Crayola® ornament from 1990.

# Spring Collection

Hallmark Crayola®
Pastel Bunny with
Egg from the 1990s.

*Crayola® Bunny*, a
Hallmark Crayola®
ornament from 1992.

*Colorful Spring*, a
Hallmark Crayola®
ornament from 1993.

*Picture Perfect*, a
Hallmark Crayola®
ornament from 1995.

Left: *Hippity-Hop Delivery*, a Hallmark Crayola® ornament from 1996.

Right: *Eggs-Pert Artist*, a Hallmark Crayola® ornament from 1997.

Hallmark Crayola® Bunny Figurines
from 1990 to 1993.

# Other Hallmark Miniatures

Six Miniature Hallmark Crayola® Bears, circa the 1990s.

Hallmark Crayola®
*Booker Beanie*
from 2000.

Hallmark Crayola®
*Booker Bear* from
2002.

Hallmark Crayola® *Bee Bright*
from 2001.

Hallmark Crayola® Snowglobe
from 1999.

# More Miniature Collectibles

Miniature Crayola® Crayon boxes, from 2000.

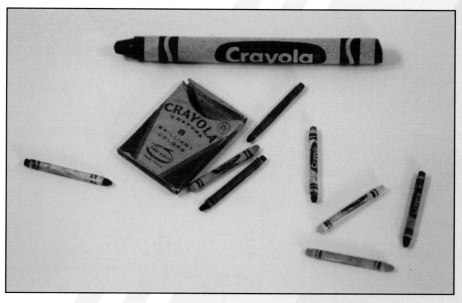

Miniature Crayola® Crayon box with eight removable crayons, by Darrel Irwin, from 2002. The box is approximately 1in x 1½in (3cm x 4cm).

## Chapter 13

# Paints and Paint Tins

## Paint Tins and Trays

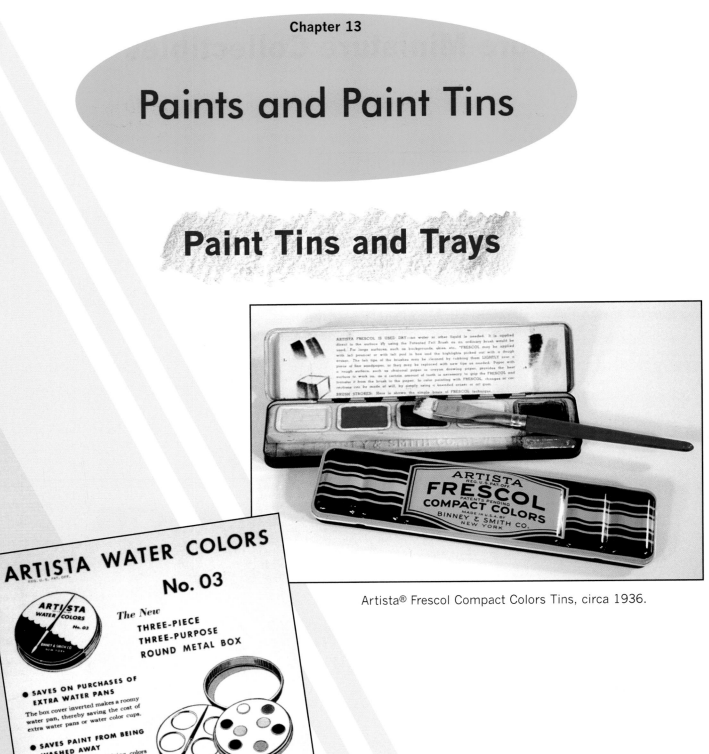

Artista® Frescol Compact Colors Tins, circa 1936.

An original advertisement from *The Drawing Teacher* for Artista® Water Colors in the round metal box, No. 03, circa 1939.

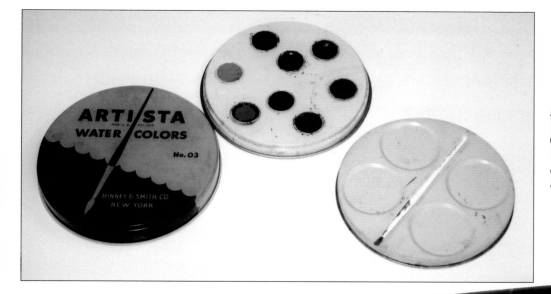

Artista® Water Colors in the round tin, No. 03, circa 1939 to the 1940s. *Photograph courtesy of Sharon Sanford.*

A Playtime Water Colors Tray in blue, circa 1940s.

An inside view of the Playtime Water Colors Tray.

A dark green Water Colors Tin, No. 510, from 1941.

An inside view of the green Water Colors Tin.

A Playtime Water Colors
Tin in red, circa 1940s.

Above: Two Arcadian Water Color
Tins, No. 525, from 1940 to the
1950s.

Left: An Artista® Water Colors Tin,
circa 1948.

Two blue and beige
Artista® Water Color Tins,
circa 1953. The double tin
is No. 16 and the single
tin is No. 09.

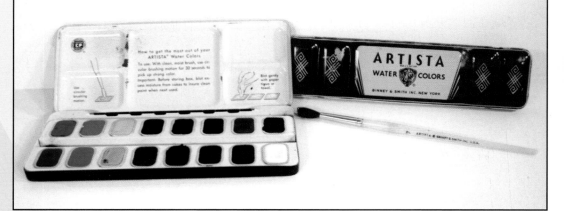

A Playtime Water Colors
Tin, No. 515, from 1957.

A Crayola® Water Colors Plastic Box, No. 080, circa 1959.

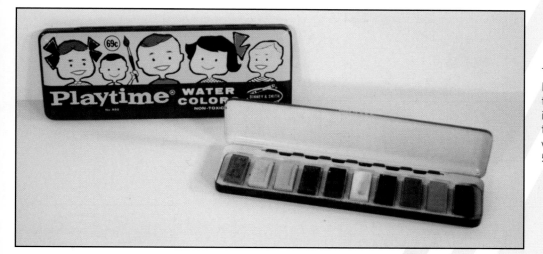

A Peacock® Water Colors Plastic Box, No. 525, from 1959 to the 1960s. *Photograph courtesy of Sharon Sanford.*

Two blue and yellow Playtime Water Colors tins, from 1960. No. 550, in the back, is a double tin and sold for 69 cents while the single tin, No. 515, sold for 29 cents.

An Artista® Water Colors Tin, No. 08, from 1960s.

A "New" Artista® Opaque Water Colors Tin, No. 508, from 1960s.

# Other Paints

A box of Artista® Flexola Paint Samples, circa 1948.

An Artista® Powder Paint Canister from 1953.

Genie Handipaint Canisters from 1953.

A Crayola® Finger Paint Powder Canister, No. 1800, from 1958 to the 1970s.

## Chapter 14

# Pins and Magnets

## Pins

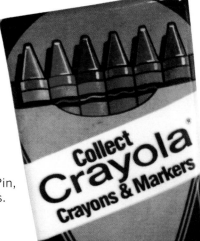

A "Collect Crayola®" Pin, circa 1980s.

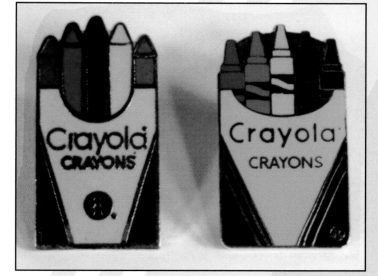

Two Crayola® Lapel Pins from the 1990s.

Two Crayola® Crayon Box Pins, circa 1995 and 1998.

*Illustrative purposes only.*

*Illustrative purposes only.*

Two Crayola® United States Postal Service Stamp Lapel Pins, circa 1998.

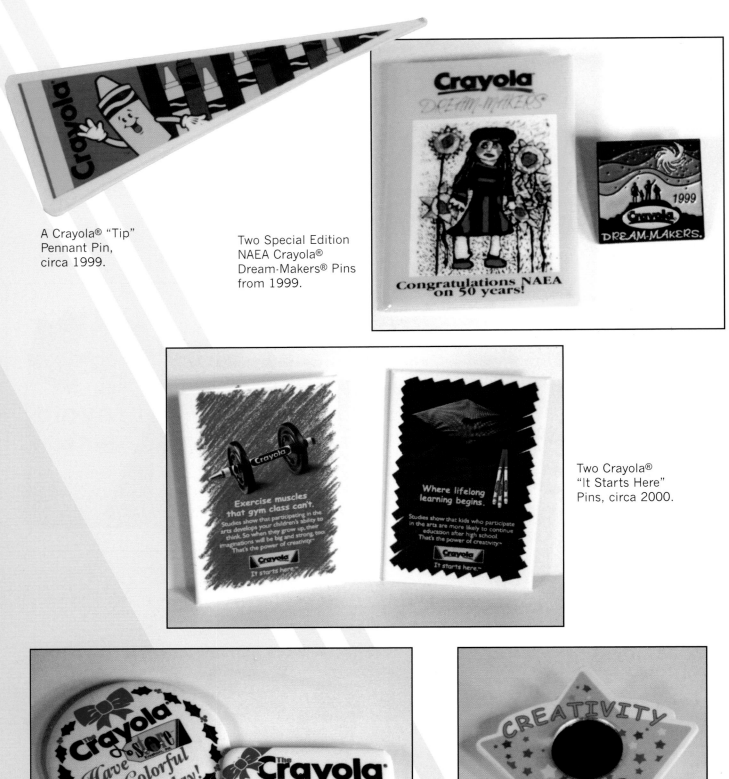

A Crayola® "Tip"
Pennant Pin,
circa 1999.

Two Special Edition
NAEA Crayola®
Dream-Makers® Pins
from 1999.

Two Crayola®
"It Starts Here"
Pins, circa 2000.

Two Crayola® Store Holiday Pins from 2001.

A Crayola® Star Pin from 2001.

# Magnets

Two Crayola® Crayon Box Magnets from the 1990s.

*Illustrative purposes only.*

*Illustrative purposes only.*

*Illustrative purposes only.*

Two Crayola® United States Postal Service Stamp Magnets from 1998.

A Crayola® Box Foam Magnet from 1999.

"Tip" in a Crayola® Airplane Foam Magnet from 1999.

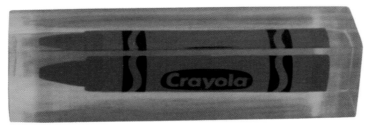

An Acrylic Crayola® Crayon Magnet from 1999.

A Crayola® Crayon Frame Magnet from 1999 with a Crayola® United States Postal Service Stamp Eraser from 1998.

Illustrative purposes only.

Crayola® Pastel Crayon Magnets from 1999.

A Red "Tip" Magnet from 1999.

## Chapter 15

# Puzzles

*Shades of Childhood!* and *Crayola®* *Freeway!* puzzles from the 1980s.

*Color Your World* puzzle from 1983 with a *Crayola®* *School Days* puzzle from 1994.

*Bears Brigade* puzzle, circa 1996.

*Octopus Under the Ocean,* a Crayola® Jigsaw Puzzle, circa 1990s.

*Crayola® Castle,* a Crayola® Jigsaw Puzzle, circa 1990s.

A FREE Crayola® Factory Puzzle from 1992.

The front view of the Hallmark puzzle *Crayola® Clownin' Around* ornament from 1999.

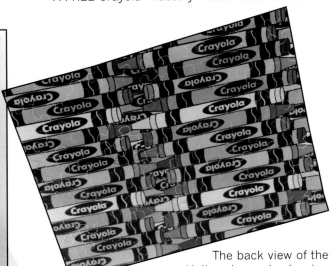

The back view of the Hallmark puzzle showing *Crayola® Crayons*, from 1999.

Right: A Crayola® Crayon Jigsaw Puzzle sold at Hallmark stores in a box resembling a box of Crayola® Crayons, from 1999.

# Tins - Old and New

### AN-DU-SEPTIC
#### DUSTLESS BLACKBOARD CRAYON

AN-DU-SEPTIC dustless crayons are made in round, square and hexagonal shapes. White only. Packed one gross sticks in a metal box as shown above. For further description of these crayons see page 25. 25 gross in a case. Weight per case, 102 lbs.

**No. 6120**—AN-DU-SEPTIC dustless crayon in a small package, twelve sticks. See page 21 for further description and illustration.

An original advertisement for An-Du-Septic® Dustless Blackboard Crayons from a 1930s issue of *Crayons, Chalks, Water Colors*. The crayons came in this tin from 1928 to the 1940s.

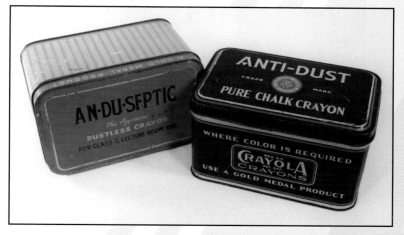

An·Du·Septic® Dustless and Pure Chalk Crayon Tins, from the 1930s to the 1940s.

Right: Vintage Colored Drawing Crayon Tins.

A Colored Crayons Tin, circa 1927.

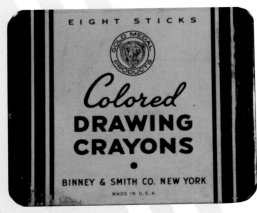
A Colored Drawing Crayons Tin from 1941.

A Colored Drawing Crayons Tin from 1953.

An 8 Brilliant Colored Crayons Tin from 1948 to the 1960s.

An assortment of Collectible Crayola® Tins.

Gold Medal "Crayola®" School Crayons Tins, No. 8, from 1982, 1985 and 1998.

A rare Crayola® Hot Air Balloon Tin from 1983 as shown in an advertisement in the Smithsonian Archives Binney & Smith Collection. *Photograph used with permission of Binney & Smith.*

Crayola® Circus Pedestal Tin from 1989.

A "Crayola®" Collector's Colors Limited Edition Tin from 1991.

A Crayola® Marker Parker Tin from 1990.

A Crayola® Crayon Tin from 1991.

A Crayola® Christmas Tin from 1992.

A "Crayola®" Childhood Memories Tin from 1994.

A Crayola® 90th Anniversary Tin from 1993.

A Crayola® 64 Tin from 1995.

A Crayola® World of Coloring Fun Tin from 1995.

A Canadian Crayola® NBA (National Basketball Association) Tin from 1995.

A Canadian Crayola® NHL (National Hockey League) Tin from 1995.

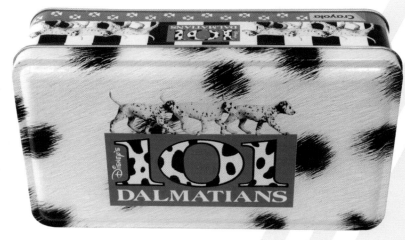

A Canadian Crayola® 101 Dalmatians Tin from 1996.

A Crayola® Peace Tin from 1995.

A Crayola® Crayons Honors the True Blue Heroes Tin from 1997.

A Crayola® "Caldor" Tin from 1997.

A Crayola® Colorful Jungle Tin from 1997.

A 16 Crayola® Colour Keeper Tin and a Crayola® 16 Crayons Á La Cire Tin, from 1997.

Crayola® Limited Edition Discovery Tins, Nos. 1 through 3, from 1997 to 2000.

Crayola® Limited Edition Discovery Tins, Nos. 4 through 6, from 1997 to 2000.

A Crayola® Arctic Tin from 1998.

A 40th Anniversary Crayola®
Crayons 64 Box Limited Edition
Tin from 1998.

A Crayola® Big Box of Ideas
Tin from 1998.

Left: A Crayola® Christmas Carols
Tin from 1999.

A Crayola® School Bus with "Tips" Tin from 1999.

A Crayola® Time Capsule Tin from 1999.

A Crayola® 52 Ultimate Pencil Collection Tin from Europe from the 1990s.

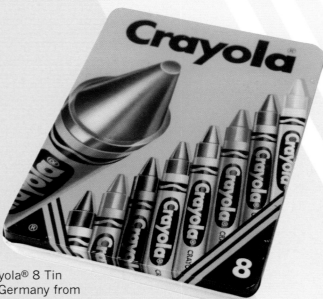

A Crayola® 8 Tin from Germany from the 1990s.

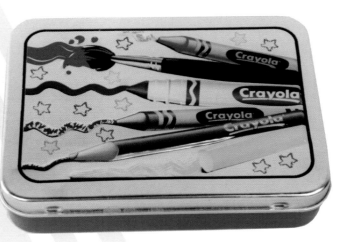

A Crayola® Art Tools Playing Cards Tin from the 1990s.

A Crayola® and Dole Fun Shapes Tin from 2000.

Front view of a Crayola® Crayons 64 Tin Bank from 2000.

Back view of the Crayola® Crayons 64 Tin Bank.

A scattered Crayola® Crayons Tin from 2000.

Right: A No. 8 "Crayola®" Gold Medal School Crayons Tin from 2000.

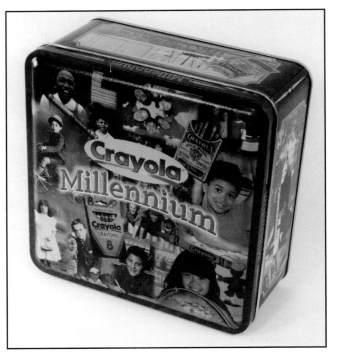

A Crayola® "Draw What?" Drawing Charades Game Tin from 2000.

A Crayola® Millennium Tin from 2000.

Left: Front view of a Crayola® Christmas Tin Bank from 2001.

Below: Back view of the Crayola® Christmas Tin Bank from 2001, shown with an original advertisement from *The Art Educationist* from 1951.

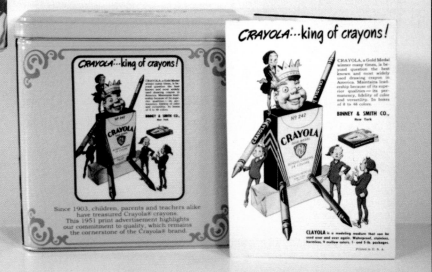

## Chapter 17

# Vehicles

Above: A Crayola® Van by Corgi from 1986.

Left: A Crayola® Delivery Car Bank from the 1990s.

A Crayola® School Bus Crayon Holder from 1993.

A Crayola® 1903 Replica Train Crayon Holder from 1994.

A Crayola® Jeep Crayon Holder from 1994.

A Crayola® Crayon Activity Train Set by Lionel from 1994.

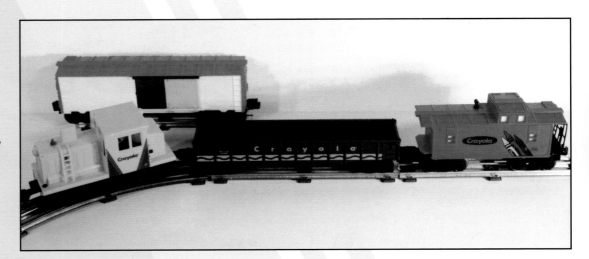

Crayola® Tractor Trailers from 1992 to 1998. *Photograph courtesy of Sharon Sanford.*

Above: A 1998 replica NASCAR Binney & Smith Racing Stock Car, in 1:24 scale.

Left: A 1998 replica NASCAR Crayola® Racing Stock Car, in 1:64 scale.

Replicas of 1940s to 1950s Ford and Chevrolet Pedal Driven Cars by Gearbox from 1998.

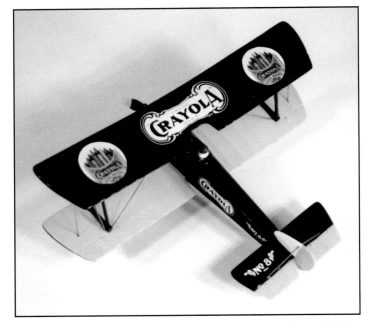

A Crayola® Crayon 1917 Sopwith Pup Airplane from 1999.

Above: A replica of a 1903 Crayola® Delivery Car, Series 1, from 1998.

Right: Replicas of 1912 Crayola® Delivery Cars, Series 2 and 3, from 1998.

A customized HO Train Set from Eckerd, from 2001.

# Part III: Crayola® Crayons Through the Years

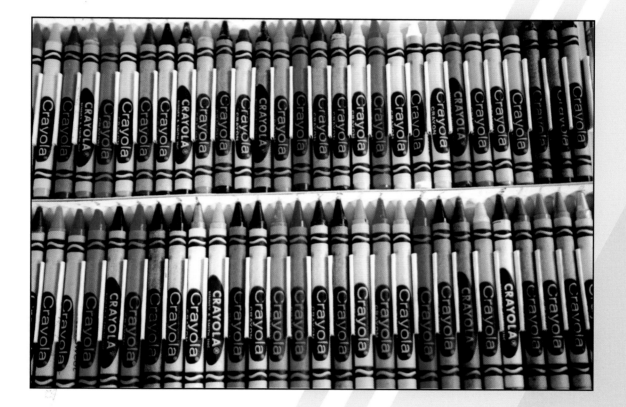

## Chapter 18

# Crayola® Crayons Archives

Since 1903, when Binney & Smith introduced the first Crayola® Crayon, people have been fascinated with the heritage of the various color names. In order to make more crayons available to more children, the company has expanded its range of colors and streamlined its production methods over the years. You may know that there are 120 core Crayola® Crayon colors, but did you know that Binney & Smith introduced more than 400 different crayon colors in their 100-year history? Search the crayon database at www.Crayola.com to find all about your favorite crayons.

### 8 Colors Available Beginning 1903

| Black | Brown | Orange | Violet | Blue | Green | Red | Yellow |
|-------|-------|--------|--------|------|-------|-----|--------|

### 48 Colors Available 1949 to 1957

| Apricot | Gold | Orange | Silver |
|---------|------|--------|--------|
| Bittersweet | Gray | Orange Red | Spring Green |
| Black | Green | Orange Yellow | Tan |
| Blue | Green Blue | Orchid | Thistle |
| Blue Green | Green Yellow | Periwinkle | Turquoise Blue |
| Blue Violet | Lemon Yellow | Pine Green | Violet (Purple) |
| Brick Red | Magenta | Prussian Blue* | Violet Blue |
| Brown | Mahogany | Red | Violet Red |
| Burnt Sienna | Maize | Red Orange | White |
| Carnation Pink | Maroon | Red Violet | Yellow |
| Cornflower | Melon | Salmon | Yellow Green |
| Flesh** | Olive Green | Sea Green | Yellow Orange |

*Name changed to "Midnight Blue" in 1958 in response to teachers' requests.

**Name voluntarily changed to "Peach" in 1962, partially as a result of the United States Civil Rights Movement.

## 64 Colors Available 1958 to 1971

All colors previously listed plus the following colors added in 1958.

| | | | |
|---|---|---|---|
| Aquamarine | Copper | Lavender | Raw Sienna |
| Blue Gray | Forest Green | Mulberry | Raw Umber |
| Burnt Orange | Goldenrod | Navy Blue | Sepia |
| Cadet Blue | Indian Red*** | Plum | Sky Blue |

***"Indian Red" is renamed "Chestnut" in 1999 in response to educators' requests who felt some children wrongly perceived the crayon color was intended to represent the skin color of Native Americans. The name originated from a reddish-brown pigment found near India commonly used in fine artist oil paint.

## 72 Colors Available 1972 to 1989

All colors previously listed plus the following fluorescent colors added in 1972.

| | | | |
|---|---|---|---|
| Atomic Tangerine | Hot Magenta | Outrageous Orange | Shocking Pink |
| Blizzard Blue | Laser Lemon | Screamin' Green | Wild Watermelon |

## 80 Colors Available 1990 to 1992

All colors previously listed plus the following fluorescent colors added in 1990.

| | | | |
|---|---|---|---|
| Electric Lime | Purple Pizzazz | Razzle Dazzle Rose | Unmellow Yellow |
| Magic Mint | Radical Red | Sunglow | Neon Carrot |

**In 1990, eight colors were retired and replaced by eight new shades.**

| Retired Colors | Replacement Colors |
|---|---|
| Green Blue | Cerulean |
| Orange Red | Vivid Tangerine |
| Orange Yellow | Jungle Green |
| Violet Blue | Fuchsia |
| Maize | Dandelion |
| Lemon Yellow | Teal Blue |
| Blue Gray | Royal Purple |
| Raw Umber | Wild Strawberry |

Retired colors were enshrined in the Crayola® Hall of Fame on August 7, 1990.

## 96 Colors Available 1993

In 1993, 16 new colors were added, named by consumers.

| | |
|---|---|
| Asparagus | Razzmatazz |
| Cerise | Robin's Egg Blue |
| Denim | Shamrock |
| Granny Smith Apple | Tickle Me Pink |
| Macaroni and Cheese | Timber Wolf |
| Mauvelous | Tropical Rain Forest |
| Pacific Blue | Tumbleweed |
| Purple Mountain's Majesty | Wisteria |

## 120 Colors Available 1998

In 1998, 24 new colors were added.

| | | | |
|---|---|---|---|
| Almond | Canary | Fern | Pink Flamingo |
| Antique Brass | Caribbean Green | Fuzzy Wuzzy Brown | Purple Heart |
| Banana Mania | Cotton Candy | Manatee | Shadow |
| Beaver | Cranberry | Mountain Meadow | Sunset Orange |
| Blue Bell | Desert Sand | Outer Space | Torch Red |
| Brink Pink | Eggplant | Pig Pink | Vivid Violet |

In addition, Binney & Smith produced several assortments of specialty crayons.

## Colors Available 2000

All colors previously listed with the following exceptions:
"Thistle" was removed from the 120-count assortment to make room for "Indigo";
"Torch Red" was renamed "Scarlet."

Note: Crayola® Crayon Chronology is based on information compiled from company records and internal sources. Additional information about the color chronology can be found at the Crayola® Web site: www.Crayola.com.

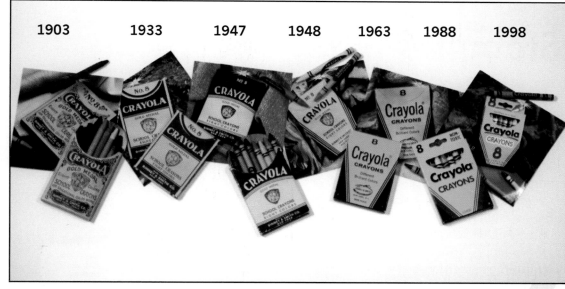

Timeline of Crayola® boxes from 1903 to 1998, with photographs from the 2000 Millennium Tin Booklet.

Back Views of Crayola® Boxes from 1903 to 1963.

## Chapter 19

# Crayola® Crayons: Stamped Into History

On January 17, 1998, a new 32-cent postage stamp was introduced to commemorate the treasured place of Crayola® Crayons in American history. The stamp was unveiled at The Crayola FACTORY® at Two Rivers Landing in Easton, Pennsylvania, as part of the "Celebrate the Century" program. The United States Postal Service featured the 1903 Crayola® Gold Medal box of eight crayons, along with twenty-nine others in the series, in an effort to recognize "the most memorable and significant people, places, events, and trends in each decade of the 20th century." The stamp was issued on February 3 at a special ceremony in Washington, D.C.

Illustrative purposes only.

The first box of **Crayola®** **crayons** was produced in 1903. It cost five cents and contained eight colors: black, brown, blue, red, violet, orange, yellow and green.

CELEBRATE THE CENTURY – 1900s

Front and back views of the Crayola® United States Postal Service "Celebrate the Century" Stamp from 1998. *Used with permission from Binney & Smith.*

A Crayola® United States Postal Service "Celebrate the Century" Stamp First Day of Issue (February 3, 1998) original stamped envelope from the Smithsonian Archives Binney & Smith Collection. *Photograph used with permission of Binney & Smith.*

Illustrative purposes only.

Illustrative purposes only.

Three versions of hand-painted Crayola® United States Postal Service "Celebrate the Century" Stamp First Day of Issue (February 3, 1998) envelopes.

## Chapter 20

# Crayola® Trivia

## Little known facts from the annals of Crayola® history. . .

Cousins Edwin Binney and C. Harold Smith began the partnership of Binney & Smith in 1885 to sell carbon black and other pigments used in various industries.

The first box of Crayola® crayons was sold in 1903 for a nickel and included the same colors available in the eight-count box today: Black, Brown, Blue, Red, Violet, Orange, Yellow and Green.

The name Crayola® was coined by Alice Binney, wife of company founder Edwin, and a former schoolteacher. She combined the words *craie,* which is French for chalk, and *ola,* for oleaginous, because crayons are made from pertroleum-based paraffin.

Renowned "American Gothic" artist Grant Wood entered a Crayola® coloring contest in the early 1900s and won. Wood later commented that winning the contest gave him the encouragement he needed to pursue a career in art.

The average child in the United States will wear down 730 crayons by his tenth birthday (or 11.4 boxes of 64s).

According to a report published by the *Christian Science Monitor,* parents buy enough crayons in a year to make a giant crayon 35 feet in diameter and 100 feet taller than the Statue of Liberty!

Kids, ages two to eight, spend an average of 28 minutes each day coloring. Combined, children in the United States spend 6.3 billion hours coloring annually, almost 10,000 human lifetimes!

Crayon color names rarely change. However, there are exceptions. In 1958, "Prussian Blue" was changed to "Midnight Blue" in response to teacher recommendations that children could no longer relate to Prussian history. In 1962, the color "Flesh" was changed to "Peach," recognizing that not everyone's flesh is the same shade.

A "Flesh" Crayola® Crayon from 1949 to 1961.

In 1959, the 72 Crayola® Crayon gift box was introduced. However, due to last minute package improvements, it actually contained 73 crayons: 64 colors plus duplicates – four reds, three blues and two blacks!

In 1990, after 37 years of service, Crayola® products' most senior crayon maker, Emerson Moser, retired after molding a record 1.4 billion crayons. It was not until his retirement that he revealed a very well-kept secret – he was actually colorblind.

The Crayola® brand name is recognized by 99 percent of Americans and is ranked 51st of all world brands (1991 Landor Image Power Survey) in terms of the brand's recognizability and consumers' esteem for the brand.

In 1993, for the first time, consumers were invited to name 16 new Crayola® crayon colors. Nearly two million suggestions were received. The 16 individuals whose names were chosen ranged in age from five to 89. Their names and ages later appeared on the crayons they named for a limited time. The 16 new color names included: Purple Mountain's Majesty, Razzmatazz, Timber Wolf, Shamrock, Cerise, Pacific Blue, Asparagus, Tickle Me Pink, Wisteria, Denim, Granny Smith Apple, Mauvelous, Tumbleweed, Robin's Egg Blue, Macaroni and Cheese and Tropical Rain Forest.

More than 100 billion Crayola® Crayons have been made since 1903. In February 1996, the 100 billionth Crayola® Crayon was made by Fred Rogers of television's "Mister Rogers' Neighborhood." The crayon was a once-in-a-lifetime color – Blue Ribbon – of which one million special 100 billionth commemorative crayons were made and sold in special commemorative boxes.

Darlene Martin, a grandmother from Port Orchard, Washington, won the actual 100 billionth Crayola® Crayon through a contest and sold it back to Binney & Smith for a $100,000 bond. The 100 billionth crayon now resides in the Crayola® Hall of Fame in downtown Easton, Pennsylvania.

A front view of the 100 billionth Crayola® Crayon.

Back view of the 100 billionth Crayola® Crayon.

On July 16, 1996, Easton, Pennsylvania, home of Crayola® crayons, hosted Crayola® ColorJam '96 – the largest gathering of people with color in their names. More than 40,000 colorful people came out for the day – including ColorJam Grand Marshal Larry Holmes and Easton Mayor Tom Goldsmith!

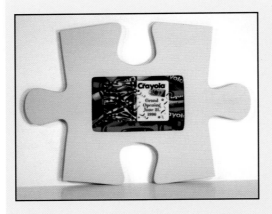

The Crayola FACTORY® at Two Rivers Landing opened in Easton, Pennsylvania, on July 16, 1996. First day attendance was approximately 8,000 people. The 100,000th visitor was seven-year-old Marshall Rein, on October 25, 1996.

Left: A Commemorative Phone Card from the Grand Opening of The Crayola® FACTORY®, June 21, 1996.

In October 1997, eight new crayon colors were issued commemorating people identified through the Crayola® Search for True Blue Heroes. In addition to being the first people in Crayola® history to ever have crayons issued bearing their names, the eight heroes, selected from more than 10,000 submissions, were also inducted into the Crayola® Hall of Fame. The new colors named by the True Blue Heroes included: Outer Space, Mountain Meadow, Fuzzy Wuzzy Brown, Brink Pink, Shadow, Banana Mania, Torch Red and Purple Heart.

A Crayola® Crayons True Blue Hero from 1997.

On January 17, 1998, the United States Postal Service unveiled its stamp commemorating the introduction of Crayola® Crayons in 1903. The stamp features the original eight-count box, which sold for a nickel and included Black, Brown, Blue, Red, Violet, Orange, Yellow and Green crayons.

In February 1998, the Crayola® 64-crayon box celebrated its 40th birthday with the reintroduction of its original packaging, complete with a built-in sharpener and original package graphics. To help celebrate the milestone, an actual 1958 Crayola® Crayon box and an assortment of advertising spanning the century, became part of the permanent collection of the Smithsonian Institution's National Museum of American History.

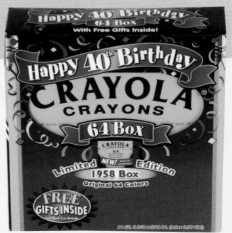

A "Happy 40th Birthday" Crayola® Crayons 64 Box Limited Edition 1958 Box, with original colors, from 1998.

In March 1999, for only the third time in Crayola® history, Binney & Smith announced plans to rename its Indian Red crayon based on feedback from educators and consumers. More than 250,000 name suggestions were received from over 100,000 colorers of all ages. Some of the most frequently suggested names were Clay Red, India Red, Sunset Red and Redwood. In the end, the new crayon name, chosen by a panel of Crayola® color experts, was Chestnut.

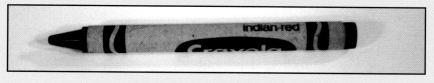

An "Indian Red" Crayola® Crayon from 1958 to 1998.

According to a Yale University study, the scent of Crayola® crayons is among the 20 most recognizable to American adults. Coffee and peanut butter are one and two. Crayola® crayons are 18.

Art materials are not the only items on which the Crayola® brand name is found. The name is licensed to more than 20 companies that make costumes, clothes, bedding, party accessories, eyeglasses and stationery items.

Crayola® is a registered trademark. However, the company permits two individuals to "borrow" the name: Crayola Walker of Bellow Falls, Vermont, and Crayola Collins of Pulaski County, Virginia.

The private crayon collection of Dr. William Mahaffey of Sandusky, Ohio, is perhaps the largest on record. The retired Navy doctor's collection boasts a spectrum of over 725 colors – all catalogued by color and manufacturer, and all sporting perfect wax points never put to paper!

Douglas Mehrens uses more crayons annually than anyone else in the world. The Phoenix-based artist goes through about 24,000 a year, many of them melted, to complete his contemporary abstract works.

Crayola® products are still manufactured in Easton, Pennsylvania (world headquarters), as well as in England and Mexico, and are sold in more than 80 countries from the island of Iceland to the tiny Central American nation of Belize. They are packaged in 12 languages: English, French, Dutch, German, Italian, Spanish, Portuguese, Danish, Finnish, Japanese, Swedish and Norwegian.

Most Crayola® crayon color names are taken from the United States Commerce Department's National Bureau of Standards book called *Color: Universal Language and Dictionary Names*. Many crayon names are also borrowed from traditional artists' paints.

Binney & Smith, maker of Crayola® products, produces nearly three billion crayons each year, an average of 12 million daily. That is enough to circle the globe six times!

Crayola® crayons come in three sizes: regular, large and Kid's First®; and three styles: regular, washable and specialty crayons.

Crayola® Crayons are made in several different sizes including boxes of 8, 16, 24, 32, 48, 64, 96 and 120. (Boxes of 3, 4, 6 and 12 Crayola® Crayons have been made.)

Although the 64 and 96 boxes are larger, the 24-count Crayola® box is the best seller.

Crayola® box sizes are in accordance with industry standards set by the Art & Craft Material Institute to minimize confusion by consumers. Crayon stick sizes – 3-5/8 inches by 5/16 inch – are also fairly standardized for the same reason.

Crayola® Crayons are made from paraffin wax and colored pigments.

In addition to making crayons, each year Binney & Smith makes 540 million Crayola® colored pencils, 425 million markers, 90 million sticks of chalk, eight million Silly Putty® eggs and 1.5 million jars of paint.

On January 31, 2001, the results of Binney & Smith's first online poll of consumer's favorite Crayola® Crayon colors were revealed. After counting more than 25,000 votes cast by Crayola® fans of all ages in the Crayola® Color Census 2000, the final tally revealed that Americans' favorite Crayola® color is blue. Six other shades of blue finished in the Top Ten including Cerulean, Midnight Blue, Aquamarine, Periwinkle, Denim and Blizzard Blue. Other colors rounding out the Top Ten list included Purple Heart, Caribbean Green and Cerise.

Favorite crayon colors of celebrities include: Robin's Egg Blue (Britney Spears); Red (Courtney Cox Arquette); Wild Strawberry (Tiger Woods); Pig Pink (Mario Andretti); Caribbean Green (Al Roker); Burnt Sienna (Billy Crystal); Blue Bell (George W. Bush); Magenta (Whoopi Goldberg); Cerulean (Katie Couric); Blue (Mike Myers); Dandelion (Candice Bergen); and Lemon Yellow (Fred Rogers of "Mr. Rogers' Neighborhood").

Crayola® Crayons currently come in 120 colors including 23 reds, 20 greens, 19 blues, 16 purples, 14 oranges, 11 browns, eight yellows, two grays, two coppers, two blacks, one white, one gold and one silver. Although Crayola® Crayons come in 120 different colors, the labels are only made in 18 colors, which cover the full color spectrum.

If all the regular size Crayola® Crayons made in one year were laid end to end on the Equator – you are right, they would melt! However, those melted bands of color would circle the Earth six times.

Binney & Smith is a subsidiary of Hallmark Cards, Inc., Kansas City, Missouri.

The year 2003 was designated as the "Centennial" of Crayola® crayons.

Note: Crayola® Trivia is based on information compiled from company records and internal sources. Additional information can be found at the Crayola® Web site: www.Crayola.com.

# Part IV:
# A Collector's Guide to Crayola® Collectibles

The Binney & Smith Company did not begin placing dates on most of their products until the early 1980s. Dates for many of these items have been found in early sales catalogs, Binney & Smith publications, and other sources from the Smithsonian Archives.

## Category: ADVERTISEMENTS

| ITEM | MANUFACTURER | YEAR | DESCRIPTION | ESTIMATED VALUE |
|------|--------------|------|-------------|-----------------|
| "$600 in Prizes – Crayola® Drawing Contest" Ad | Binney & Smith | 1918 | Black and white ad with picture of boy and girl, advertises the 1903 box of crayons. Includes rules, ages and prizes (Liberty Bond and War Savings Stamps). | $20-$30 |
| Binney & Smith Calendar Blotters | Binney & Smith | 1926-1927 | Calendars with seasonal themes and "words of wisdom," made each month during the mid-1920s. (Back of calendar is ink blotter.) | $10-$20 |
| Crayola® Ad – Christmas Tree | Binney & Smith | 1927 | Black and white ad in December 1927 magazine, features picture of tree and presents. "What is wrong with this Christmas Tree?" | $10-$15 |
| *The Drawing Teacher* Ads | Binney & Smith | 1935-1948 | Various Binney & Smith products advertised on the back cover of each pamphlet of *The Drawing Teacher*. | $10-$15 |
| *The Art Educationist* Ads | Binney & Smith | 1949-1953 | Various Binney & Smith products advertised on the back cover of each pamphlet of *The Art Educationist*. | $10-$15 |
| Crayola® Advertising Blotter | Binney & Smith | circa 1950 | Blotter with elf and Crayola® crayons with color graphics. Ad is for Helena Office Supply Co., Helena, Montana. (Back of ad is ink blotter). | $15-$25 |
| Crayola® Advertising Blotter | Binney & Smith | 1953 | "50 Years of Crayola® Leadership" blotter with "rainbow of crayon colors" graphics. Ad is for Brown Specialty Company, Galesburg, Illinois. (Back of ad is ink blotter). | $15-$25 |
| Magazine Ad – "Crayola® for Healthy Fun" | Binney & Smith | 1957 | Small black and white ad shows little girl coloring. Advertises box of forty-eight crayons and the *Crayola® Craft Book*. | $10-$15 |
| Crayola® Box Display Sign | Binney & Smith | circa 1958 | Cardboard sign looks like a dark green and yellow Crayola® box. Has cardboard easel-back so that it can stand alone. Measures 12in x 7½in (31cm x 19cm). | $20-$30 |
| Magazine Ad – "Give Crayola® '64'..." | *Family Circle* Binney & Smith | 1958 | Color ad reads "Give Crayola® '64' with the Built-In Sharpener 64 crayons 64 colors. Only $1.00." | $10-$15 |
| Magazine Ad – Crayola® Advertisement | Binney & Smith | circa 1962 | "Awakening to the Wonderful World of Color... *remember*?" Color ad of little girl drawing with box of eight Crayola® crayons. | $10-$15 |

| ITEM | MANUFACTURER | YEAR | DESCRIPTION | ESTIMATED VALUE |
|---|---|---|---|---|
| Magazine Ad – Crayola® Advertisement | *Good Housekeeping* Binney & Smith | circa 1965 | "Bring home a nice fresh box of Crayola® crayons today. For a lot of reasons." Color ad shows an old cigar box with broken crayons and four sizes of new Crayola® crayon boxes available (8, 16, 48, 64). | $10-$15 |
| Note: Numerous advertisements for Crayola® Crayons can be found in a variety of publications at comparable prices. | | | | |
| FREE! Crayola® Crayons | *Binney & Smith Double Cola* | circa 1970 | Dark green and yellow cardboard hanging package contains three Crayola® crayons and advertises Double Cola. Back has clown bookmark to color. | $10-$15 |
| CosMc! Crayola® | *Binney & Smith McDonald's* | 1987 | Happy Meal prize includes two large Crayola® crayons in sealed bag. Made for children under three. | $5-$10 |
| McDonald's CosMc Crayola® Happy Meal | *Binney & Smith McDonald's* | 1987 | CosMc Happy Meal box has a variety of activities for kids. | $5-$10 |
| *Rainbow Reporter* Ad | *Binney & Smith* | 1988 | Color ad features "Crayola® Crayon Packages" from 1903 to 1988. Includes nine different package designs. | $10-$20 |
| 3-D Crayola® Advertising Box | *Binney & Smith* | circa 1993 | Giant cardboard display box of Crayola® crayons used by Binney & Smith for exhibits. Measures 24in x 36in x 10in (61cm x 91cm x 25cm). | $20-$30 |
| "Crayola® – It Starts Here" Ads | *Binney & Smith* | 2000 | Recent Crayola® advertising campaign ads emphasize the importance of arts education to a child's overall development and learning. | $3-$5 |

# Category: ART

| ITEM | MANUFACTURER | YEAR | DESCRIPTION | ESTIMATED VALUE |
|---|---|---|---|---|
| *Crayola® Crayons Poster* Artist: Mickey Myers | *Choice Editions* | 1979 | Colorful poster art with rows of large Crayola® crayons, printed in San Francisco. Approximately 41in x 27in (104cm x 69cm). | $25-$35 |
| *Crayola® Crayon Box Poster* Artist: Mickey Myers | *Choice Editions* | 1979 | Colorful poster art with box of Crayola® crayons, printed in San Francisco. 39in x 25in (98cm x 64cm). | $25-$35 |
| *Crayola® Tie* | *Binney & Smith* | circa 1981 | Original artwork from the Smithsonian Archives Binney & Smith Collection, features several watercolor paintings of ties to be marketed. (Actual size of tie.) | NFS |
| "Crayon Boxes" Artist: Kate Nessler | *Commissioned by Binney & Smith* | 1984 | Limited edition print of original watercolor with two Crayola® crayon boxes and broken crayons scattered over child's artwork. 12½in x 19½in (32cm x 50cm). | $75-$100 |
| *Uncle Sam with Crayola® Crayons* | *Binney & Smith* | circa 1987 | This original painting, from the Smithsonian Archives Binney & Smith Collection, was used in a 1987 Crayola® ad "We will protect our good name." Painting is approximately 20in x 16in (51cm x 41cm). | NFS |
| *Crayola® Crayon Scarf* | *Binney & Smith* | 1990s | Crayola® crayons scarves are available in several styles. The one featured in this book has been framed and used as a work of art. Approximately 30in x 30in (76cm x 76cm). | $30-$35 |
| "Six Crayola® Crayons" Artist: Mickey Myers | *Myers Exhibition Gallery 92* | 1991 | Handmade acrylic wall hanging features six Crayola® crayons. Approximately 25in x 17in (64cm x 43). | $50-$75 |
| "Color Spills" Artist: Gail Farrell | *Courtesy of the Photographer* | circa 1995 | Color photograph of Crayola® crayons falling onto the floor in a prism of light. 6in x 4in (15cm x 10cm). | $10-$20 |
| "The Vision" Artist: Ron DeLong | *Commissioned by Binney & Smith* | 1998 | Bronze sculpture commissioned by Binney & Smith for the "Salesman of the Year" Award. Depicts family with little girl showing parents her artwork. Approximately 14in (36cm). | $300-$500 |
| Limoges "Crayola" Box with four Trinket Crayons | *Sinclair Limoges-France* | 1999 | Hand-painted porcelain hinged box depicts "Crayola" crayon box with four crayons. "Peint main Sinclair-Limoges, France, limited edition, one of 750" on box. Includes Certificate of Authenticity. 2¼in x 1½in (6cm x 4cm). | $100-$130 |
| "Crayola® Crayons" Artist: Tony Azzito | *ART4SALE.COM* | 1999 | Acrylic painting with silkscreen of 1903 box of Crayola® crayons – "Pop art in the style of Andy Warhol." 34in x 30in (86cm x 76cm). | $750-$1000 |

# Category: BOOKS and OTHER PUBLICATIONS

## Binney & Smith Publications

| ITEM | MANUFACTURER | YEAR | DESCRIPTION | ESTIMATED VALUE |
|---|---|---|---|---|
| The Art of "CRAYOLA®" Painting | Binney & Smith | 1904 | Vintage booklet bound with string with a wax seal that says "Binney & Smith Gold Medal, St. Louis 1904." The sixteen-page booklet includes photograph of original Crayola® boxes. "Price Ten Cents" on front. | $75-$100 |
| "Chalk Crayon Price List" | Binney & Smith | 1913 | Eight-page brochure includes prices for lecturers' crayons, as well as railroad and carpenters' chalks in white and assorted colors. | $15-$25 |
| "Crayons for Every Use Price List" | Binney & Smith | 1915 | Eight-page brochure includes prices for drawing crayons, slate pencils and assorted chalks. | $15-$25 |
| "Gold Medal Price List" | Binney & Smith | 1919 | Eight-page brochure includes price list for early samples of Crayola® crayons, dustless blackboard crayon, chalk, slate pencils and other items. | $15-$25 |
| Crayons, Chalks, Water Colors | Binney & Smith | 1927-1930s | Each issue of this Binney & Smith sales catalog contains approximately forty pages with color pictures of early crayons, chalks and paints. | $50-$100 |
| Artista® Water Colors | Binney & Smith | 1937 | Small booklet gives information about No. 09 Artista® Water Colors. The twelve-page booklet includes a color wheel with twelve colors. | $15-$25 |
| "Gold Medal Products School Catalogs" | Binney & Smith | 1940-1950s | Each catalog contains a price list and descriptions for all Binney & Smith products. Includes black and white graphics of old and "new" Crayola® boxes. | $15-$25 |
| "Artista® Tempera Show Card Colors" | Binney & Smith | 1941 | Brochure features black and gold Artista® paint on cover. Inside is a color wheel with samples of each color available. Back gives description of texture, sizes and uses of tempera paint. | $10-$20 |

Note: A variety of Binney & Smith brochures and booklets published between 1939 and 1941 can be found at comparable prices.

| ITEM | MANUFACTURER | YEAR | DESCRIPTION | ESTIMATED VALUE |
|---|---|---|---|---|
| The Drawing Teacher Series | Binney & Smith | 1935-1948 | Published every other month for art teachers, each folded brochure includes editorial, lesson plan for specific grade and ads for various Binney & Smith products. | $10-$15 |
| The Story of a Rainbow | Binney & Smith | 1947 | Booklet published to provide employees with information about the history and benefits of working for the Binney & Smith Company. | $30-$60 |
| "Crayola® Colored Drawing Crayon" | Binney & Smith | 1948 | Small white three-fold pamphlet printed in red with "Indian" theme demonstrates the use of crayons for stenciling, design and decoration. | $10-$15 |
| "Genie Finger Paint Powder" | Binney & Smith | 1948 | Small greenish-blue pamphlet shows directions for using and mixing Genie Finger Paint Powder. | $10-$15 |
| The Art Educationist Series | Binney & Smith | 1949-1953 | Published every other month for art teachers, each foldout pamphlet includes editorial, comments and ad for various Binney & Smith products. | $10-$15 |
| "Artista® Flexola" | Binney & Smith | 1949 | Small three-fold pamphlet printed in blue has palette of paint and elves with tube of Flexola on front. Brochure contains information about using the product. | $10-$15 |
| "Suggested Minimum List of Art Materials" | Binney & Smith | 1950 | Two-page bright yellow brochure has pictures of all Binney & Smith products for use with kindergarten through high school. Includes price list and suggested materials needed for classroom use. | $10-$15 |
| "The Place of Art in Elementary/Secondary School" | American School Board Journal Binney & Smith | 1950 | Four-page folded brochure with photographs on the importance of art in the schools, reprinted by Binney & Smith. | $10-$15 |
| "Crayola® Colored Crayon" | Binney & Smith | circa 1950 | Color chart of various Crayola® crayon boxes explains different assortments made by Binney & Smith. | $10-$15 |

| ITEM | MANUFACTURER | YEAR | DESCRIPTION | ESTIMATED VALUE |
|---|---|---|---|---|
| *The B & S Rainbow Reporter* | *Binney & Smith* | 1953 | Booklet published to celebrate the 50th anniversary of Crayola® and provide employees with information about the Binney & Smith Company. | $25-$30 |
| *Creative Crafts with Crayola®* | *Binney & Smith* | 1953 | White booklet with color graphics has elf on cover holding a large red Crayola® crayon. Booklet has thirty-one pages and contains ideas for using crayons and information about the color wheel, prices and various sizes and colors available. | $15-$20 |
| *Genie Handipaint* | *Binney & Smith* | 1953 | One-page blue front and yellow back ad with elves demonstrates how to use powdered Genie Handipaint. | $5 |
| *Shaw Finger-Paint – The Original Finger Paint* | *Binney & Smith* | 1953 | Small bright pink and white booklet contains information about Shaw Finger-Paint products. Eight-page booklet includes demonstrations and projects for using Shaw products. | $10-$15 |
| *"Artista® Powder Paint"* | *Binney & Smith* | 1953 | Green and yellow three-fold pamphlet has color chart and information about mixing and using Artista® powder paint. | $5-$10 |
| *"Gold Medal Products for Art Education" Packet of Booklets* | *Binney & Smith* | 1954 | Red and white envelope contains twelve booklets, pamphlets and brochures for Binney & Smith products. Names of different products are printed on the packet. (Each of the inserts is described in this category.) | Complete $75-$125 |
| *"Gold Medal Products" School Catalog* | *Binney & Smith* | 1954 | Gold and black booklet contains a price list and description for all Binney & Smith products. Includes black and white graphics of old and "new" Crayola® boxes. Booklet has thirty pages. | $15-$25 |
| *"Artista® Tempera"* | *Binney & Smith* | 1954 | Three-page orange and white foldout with rooster on the cover gives information about different techniques and projects for using Artista® tempera paint and an overview of the color wheel. Includes price lists for different sizes and so forth. | $5-$10 |
| *"Artista® Water Colors"* | *Binney & Smith* | 1954 | Three-page foldout has Artista® paint tin on the cover and is white with orange and blue graphics. Includes information about techniques and projects for using Artista® water colors. Includes price lists for different sizes and so forth. | $5-$10 |
| *Learning to Use Your Crayola® Crayons* | *Binney & Smith* | 1976 | Booklet contains colored pictures and drawings to demonstrate a variety of Crayola® crayon techniques and projects. | $10-$15 |
| *Apprendiendo a usar crayons Crayola® (Spanish version of Learning to Use Your Crayola® Crayons)* | *Binney & Smith* | circa 1976 | Booklet contains colored pictures and drawings to demonstrate a variety of Crayola® crayon techniques and projects. | $15-$20 |
| *Rainbow Reporter* | *Binney & Smith* | 1988 | This summer edition features Crayola® crayon box design throughout the years – "Why Change An American Classic?" | $15-$25 |
| *Crayola® Art Techniques* | *Binney & Smith* | 1991 | Booklet describes a variety of techniques for using Crayola® products such as crayons, colored pencils, paints and markers. Includes sixteen pages of color pictures and a history and timeline of Binney & Smith. | $10-$20 |
| *Rainbow Reporter* | *Binney & Smith* | 1993 | This winter edition features Crayola® crayon licensing – "New Horizons for the Crayola® trademark." | $15-$25 |

Note: The *Rainbow Reporter* is a periodical for Binney & Smith employees dating back to the 1950s.

| ITEM | MANUFACTURER | YEAR | DESCRIPTION | ESTIMATED VALUE |
|---|---|---|---|---|
| *Watch It Made in the U.S.A.* Authors: Karen Axelrod & Bruce Brumberg | Avalon Travel Publishing | 2001 | Soft cover book is a visitor's guide to companies that make favorite products. Features Crayola® crayons on cover and foreword by Rich Gurin, former Binney & Smith CEO. | $15-$20 |

### Children's Books

| ITEM | MANUFACTURER | YEAR | DESCRIPTION | ESTIMATED VALUE |
|---|---|---|---|---|
| *Color 'n' Draw Fold-A-Book ABC* | Binney & Smith | 1977 | Children's book includes alphabet from A to Z for child to color and re-color with Easy-Off crayons. | $5-$10 |

| ITEM | MANUFACTURER | YEAR | DESCRIPTION | ESTIMATED VALUE |
|---|---|---|---|---|
| Color 'n' Draw Fold-A-Book Train & Circus Parade | Binney & Smith | 1977 | Children's book includes a train full of circus animals and performers for child to color and re-color with Easy-Off crayons. | $5-$10 |
| Color 'n' Draw Fold-A-Book Game Time | Binney & Smith | 1978 | Children's book includes a variety of word games, strategy games and puzzles that can be played by one or two players. Includes Easy-Off crayons. | $5-$10 |
| Crayola® Fold-A-Book Beautiful Seasons | Binney & Smith | 1980 | Children's book includes scenes for each season for child to color and re-color. Use with Easy-Off crayons. | $5-$10 |
| How is a Crayon Made? Author: Charles Oz | Scholastic Binney & Smith | 1988 | Hardback children's book shows how Crayola® crayons are made. Photographs of the process from beginning to end as the crayons are made in the factory. | $10-$20 |
| How is a Crayon Made? Author: Charles Oz | Scholastic Binney & Smith | 1988 | (Soft cover version of the book above.) | $5-$10 |
| Crayola® Bunny Saves the Day | Binney & Smith | 1990 | This pop-up book features Crayola® Painter Bunny and Candy Cotton Tail from the Spring Collection. | $10-$15 |
| Crayons from Start to Finish Author: Samuel G. Woods | Blackbirch Press Binney & Smith | 1999 | Hardback children's book shows how Crayola® crayons are made "from start to finish." Also includes brief history, timeline, glossary and Crayola® trivia. Thirty-two pages. | $10-$20 |

# Category: CHALK, PASTELS and PENCILS

**Chalk (Chalk Crayon)**
(Note: Dates are based on Binney & Smith Company records and information in the Smithsonian Archives Binney & Smith Collection. Whenever possible, a range of dates is given since some items were made for a number of years.)

| ITEM | MANUFACTURER | YEAR | DESCRIPTION | ESTIMATED VALUE |
|---|---|---|---|---|
| Binney & Smith Chalk Crayon | Binney & Smith | circa 1915 | Chalk Crayon Binney & Smith brand has red and white label with Gold Medal logo. Wooden box with slide top contains chalk crayons. "Solid color. One gross sticks." 4½in x 7in x 4in (12cm x 18cm x 10cm). | $10-$20 |
| Best School Crayon Co. | Binney & Smith | circa 1924 | Best School Crayon Yellow Enamel Trademark has stenciled lettering/no label. One gross. 4½in x 7in x 4in (12cm x 18cm x 10cm. | $10-$20 |
| Atlantic Brand Chalk | Binney & Smith | circa 1924 | Wooden box with slide top contains one gross of Atlantic brand white crayon chalk sticks. 4½in x 7in x 4in (12 cm x 18cm x 10 cm). | $10-$20 |
| UVA Chalk Crayons ("Uniform Value Assured") | Binney & Smith | circa 1924 | Wooden box with slide top contains one gross chalk crayons "softer than Binney & Smith brand." 4½in x 7in x 4in (12cm x 18cm x 10cm). | $10-$20 |
| UVA Assorted Chalk Crayons | Binney & Smith | circa 1924 | No. 702. Tiny green and white box has seven assorted chalk crayons. Approximately 2¼in x 2¼in x ¼in (6.cm x 6cm x .65cm). | $20-$25 |
| Little Folks Chalk Crayon | Binney & Smith | circa 1927 | No. 3043. Small red and white box has three sticks of UVA white chalk crayons. Back says "Made by Binney & Smith Co. New York. Gold Medal Crayons for Every Use. Made in USA." 3¼in x 1¼in x ½in (8cm x 3cm x 1cm). | $15-$25 |
| Little Folks Chalk Crayon | Binney & Smith | circa 1927 | No. 7023. Small green and white box has three sticks of UVA white chalk crayons. Back says "Made by Binney & Smith Co. New York. Gold Medal Crayons for Every Use. Made in USA." 3¼in x 1¼in x ½in (8cm x 3cm x 1cm). | $15-$25 |
| "Spectra" Pastel Crayon Box | Binney & Smith | circa 1927 | Brown slide-out box contains pastel crayons in eight colors. Made in New York, London, Paris and Hamburg. 3¾in x 2¾in x ½in (10cm x 7cm x 1cm). | $15-$25 |
| Spectra Pastel Crayon | Binney & Smith | circa 1927-1930 | No. 15. Dark gray slide-out box with black lettering has eight pastel crayons. 4in x 3in x ½in (10cm x 8cm x 1cm). | $15-$25 |

| ITEM | MANUFACTURER | YEAR | DESCRIPTION | ESTIMATED VALUE |
|---|---|---|---|---|
| *Spectra Pastel Crayons* | Binney & Smith | circa 1927-1930 | No. 21. Gold Medal Pastel Crayons in gray box with lift-off top contains twenty-one pastels in assorted colors. 8in x 3½in x ½in (20cm x 9cm x 1cm). | $15-$25 |
| *Lecturers Squares* | Binney & Smith | circa 1930s | No. 905. Box with lift-off top and red and white label has five color chalk squares. Gold Medal logo. Approximately 3in x 3½in x ½in (8cm x 9cm x 1cm). | $15-$25 |
| *Chalk Crayon* | Binney & Smith | circa 1940s | No. 318. Red and white box with row of white chalk on front contains sixteen sticks of white chalk. Gold Medal logo. 3½in x 2½in x 1¼in (9cm x 6cm x 3cm). | $5-$15 |
| *Chalk Crayon* | Binney & Smith | 1940s | No. 612. Red and beige box with cutout opening to show chalk. Twelve sticks. Back lists other Binney & Smith products: Crayola®, Crayolet, Shaw Finger-Paint, Perma, Artista®, Frescol, An-Du-Septic®. 3½in x 2½in x ¾in (9cm x 6cm x 2cm). | $5-$15 |
| *Chalk Crayon* | Binney & Smith | circa 1940-1950 | No. 812. Green and beige box with opening to show chalk. "A Gold Medal Product." Twelve sticks of pastel chalk. Back lists other Binney & Smith products: Crayola®, Crayolet, Shaw Finger-Paint, Perma, Artista®, Frescol, An-Du-Septic®. 3½in x 2½in x ¾in (9cm x 6cm x 2cm). | $5-$15 |
| *Chalk Crayon – UVA Brand* | Binney & Smith | 1940-1950 | No. 604. Small black box has navy and white label on lift-off top. UVA Brand. Twenty-four colors. Gold Medal logo. 3in x 2in x 3½in (8cm x 5cm x 9cm). | $15-$25 |
| *An-Du-Septic® Gold Medal Products* | Binney & Smith | circa 1941 | Wooden box with slide top has black and white labels on top and ends: "Highest Award Always" – Gold Medal logo and lists different brands on top of box (Anti-Dust®, Binney & Smith Brand, Pos-Ter-Art, Crayola®, Perma, Artista®.) One gross. 4½in x 6¼in x 4in (12cm x 16cm x 10cm). | $10-$20 |
| *Binney & Smith Pos-Ter-Art Wooden Box* | Binney & Smith | circa 1941 | No. 172. Wooden slide-out box with blue and white label contains seventy-two sticks of assorted colors of chalk. Approximately 8¼in x 9¼in x 3¾in (21cm x 24cm x 10cm). | $10-$20 |
| *Lecturers Chalk Crayon* | Binney & Smith | 1946 | No. 908. Small "wood grain" cardboard box has red and white label on lift-off top. UVA Brand. Eight sticks. Gold Medal logo. 4¼in x 3¼in x ¾in (11cm x 8cm x 2cm). | $10-$20 |
| *Lecturers Crayon* | Binney & Smith | 1950s | No. 912. Small black box has red and white label on lift-off top. UVA Brand. Twelve square sticks. Gold Medal logo. 3in x 2in x 3½in (8cm x 5cm x 9cm). | $15-$25 |
| *UVA Colored Chalk Crayon* | Binney & Smith | 1950-1960s | No. 816. Dark green and beige box with opening to show chalk. Sixteen sticks. Price: 15 cents. 3½in x 3¼in x 1in (9cm x 8cm x 3cm). | $5-$10 |
| *An-Du-Septic® Dustless Chalk* | Binney & Smith | circa 1958 | No. 5144. Red and orange box of dustless chalk includes twelve sticks in assorted colors. Non-toxic. 8in x 3in x ¾in (20cm x 8cm x 2cm). | $10-$15 |
| *An-Du-Septic® Dustless Chalk* | Binney & Smith | 1958 | No. 6124. Large flat red and orange box with lift-off top contains twenty-four colors. Non-toxic. "For use on paper only – For chalkboards use KLEERWAE colored dustless chalk." 6in x 8in x 1in (15cm x 20cm x 3cm). | $10-$20 |
| *Colored Chalk Crayon* | Binney & Smith | 1960s | No. 816. Navy box with white lettering has picture of chalk on front. Sixteen sticks. Top has Gold Medal logo. 3½in x 3½in x 1in (9cm x 9cm x 3cm). | $5-$10 |
| *Playtime White Chalk* | Binney & Smith | 1968 | No. 510. Blue and yellow box has picture of children and contains twelve sticks of white chalk. Price: 10 cents. 3½in x 2½in x 1in (9cm x 6cm x 3cm). | $5 |
| *Colored Chalk* | Binney & Smith | 1968 | No. 816. Green and white box contains sixteen sticks of colored chalk. Price: 15 cents. 3½in x 3½in x 1in (9cm x 9cm x 3cm). | $5-$10 |

| ITEM | MANUFACTURER | YEAR | DESCRIPTION | ESTIMATED VALUE |
|---|---|---|---|---|
| *White Chalk* | Binney & Smith | circa 1968 | No. 320. Red box with white lettering contains twenty sticks of chalk. Price: 15 cents. 3½in x 4¼in x 1in (9cm x 11cm x 3cm). | $5-$10 |
| *12 Batons Craie Blanche Swan Crayons* | Binney & Smith Canada | circa 1970 | No. 312. Blue and white box contains twelve sticks of white chalk. Made by Canada Crayon Co. Non-toxic. 3¼in x 2½in x ¾in (8cm x 6cm x 2cm). | $10-$15 |
| *Playtime White Chalk* | Binney & Smith | circa 1970 | No. 320. Red box with white lettering contains twelve sticks. Price: 15 cents. 3½in x 2½in x 1in (9cm x 6cm x 3cm). | $5-$10 |
| *Artista® Colored Poster Chalk* | Binney & Smith | 1970s | No. 136. Large aqua cardboard box has lettering on lift-off top and includes thirty-six sticks in assorted colors. "For artwork on paper only." Non-toxic. 7in x 8½in x 3in (18cm x 22cm x 8cm). | $10-$20 |
| *Crayola® An-Du-Septic® Chalk* | Binney & Smith | 1980s | No. 1400. Dark green and yellow box contains twelve sticks of white chalk. "White Low Dust Chalk – Easy to Erase." Non-toxic. 3½in x 2½in x 1in (9cm x 6cm x 3cm). | $5-$10 |

### Pastels and Pencils

| ITEM | MANUFACTURER | YEAR | DESCRIPTION | ESTIMATED VALUE |
|---|---|---|---|---|
| *Slate Pencils* | Binney & Smith | Early 1900s | Cardboard box contains fifty An-Du-Septic® slate pencils. 5½in x 1½in x 2in (14cm x 4cm x 5cm). | $50-$75 |
| *Artista® Oil Pastels* | Binney & Smith | 1964 | No. 212. Aqua and white box has red and black lettering on lift-off top. Twelve vivid colors of Artista® oil pastels. White "palette" logo. Non-toxic. 3¼in x 6in x ½in (8cm x 15cm x 1cm). | $10-$15 |
| *24 Crayola® Smooth Bright Colored Pencils* | Binney & Smith | 1987 | Dark green and yellow box includes twenty-four pre-sharpened pencils. Back shows how to use pencils to produce a variety of shades and tints and so forth. 8½in x 3¾in x ¾in (22cm x 10cm x 2cm). | $10-$15 |
| *Crayola® Coloured Pencils* | Binney & Smith Europe | circa 2000 | No. 3678. Eight wooden "coloured" pencils with "colourful" plants and animals on each one. Made in England: "Wood from renewable plantations." Back of box shows pictures being "coloured" with pencils. 7in x 5in x ¾in (18cm x 13cm x 2cm). | $10-$15 |
| *Crayola® Mes Debuts* | Binney & Smith France | circa 2000 | No. 3677. Six triangle-shaped colored pencils are for ages two plus and made "for little hands." Card (instead of box) is labeled in French. 6in x 4½in (15cm x 12cm). | $5-$10 |

## Category: CRAYONS

### Pressed Crayons
(Note: The "Crayola®" name not used on products except for molded crayons until 1978.)

| ITEM | MANUFACTURER | YEAR | DESCRIPTION | ESTIMATED VALUE |
|---|---|---|---|---|
| Staonal® Crayon No.1 | Binney & Smith | Early 1900s | No. 1. Red box contains one dozen marking crayons. "Stays on everything." 1½in x 6in x 1in (4cm x 15cm x 3cm). | $15-$25 |
| Gotham Marking Crayon | Binney & Smith | Early 1900s | No. 23. Black and yellow box contains twelve black marking crayons. Made in USA. 5¼in x 2½in x 1¾in (13cm x 6cm x 5cm). | $10-$20 |
| Tiny Tots Drawing Crayons | Binney & Smith | 1920-1930s | No. 44. Red and beige box contains eight small drawing crayons. No labels on crayons. "Artista® Water Colors" on back. 2½in x 2½in x ¼in (6cm x 6cm x .6cm). | $15-$30 |
| Little Folks Cerata Colored Crayons | Binney & Smith | circa 1927 | No. 14. Green box of colored crayons has picture of boy and girl drawing and floral design on back. 3¾in x 2¾in x ½in (10cm x 7cm x 1cm). | $20-$30 |
| Durel Crayons | Binney & Smith | circa 1928 | No. 210. Navy and yellow box with Gold Medal logo contains eight colors. Back has place for name, grade and school. 3¼in x 2-3/8in x 3/8in (8cm x 6cm x .9cm). | $15-$20 |

| ITEM | MANUFACTURER | YEAR | DESCRIPTION | ESTIMATED VALUE |
|---|---|---|---|---|
| Crayolet Colored Drawing Crayons | Binney & Smith | circa 1928 | No. 14. Red and beige box contains eight colored drawing crayons. Back reads "Crayolet and Crayola® should not be confused. Crayolet Crayons are the best in their particular class, just as Crayola® Crayons are the standard for highest quality." 3¾in x 2¾in x 3/8in (10cm x 7cm x .9cm). | $15-$20 |
| Munsell Perma Pressed Crayon | Binney & Smith | 1930s | No. 220 M. Brown and beige box contains 22 colors. "Five principal hues and five intermediate hues at middle value and middle chroma – Five principal hues and five intermediate hues at maximum chroma with middle gray and black." 4in x 7¾in x ½in (10cm x 19cm x 1cm). | $15-$25 |
| "Perma" Pressed Crayon | Binney & Smith | 1940s | No. 81. Navy and white slide-open box has eight Perma pressed crayons. 4in x 3in x ½in (10cm x 8cm x 1cm). | $15-$20 |
| Perma Pressed Crayon | Binney & Smith | circa 1940s | No. 85. Gold and brown box has lift-off lid with Gold Medal logo. Box contains sixteen Perma pressed crayons. 4in x 5½in x ½in (10cm x 14cm x 1cm). | $10-$15 |
| Perma Pressed Crayon | Binney & Smith | 1940s | No. 85. Navy blue and white striped box has lift-off lid with Gold Medal logo. Box contains 16 Perma pressed crayons. 4in x 5½in x ½in (10cm x 14cm x 1cm). | $10-$15 |
| Perma Colored Pressed Crayons | Binney & Smith | 1940s | Number 93. Navy blue and beige box contains pressed crayons in eight colors. "Use Trade Mark Artista® Water Colors" on back. 3¾in x 2¾in x 3/8in (10cm x 7cm x .9cm). | $10-$15 |
| Anti-Roll® Drawing Crayon | Binney & Smith | circa 1940s | No. 25. Red and white box has Gold Medal label. Includes eight drawing crayons. Back reads "The plano-convex contour of this crayon prevents rolling off the desk." 3¾in x 2¾in x 3/8in (10cm x 7cm x .9cm). | $10-$20 |
| Besco Gold Medal Drawing Crayons | Binney & Smith | circa 1941 | No. 10. Navy and beige box that hinges on right side has eight colors. Gold Medal logo on label. 4½in x 3¾in x ½in (12cm x 10cm x 1cm). | $15-$20 |
| Crayolet Colored Drawing Crayons | Binney & Smith | 1940-1950s | No. 32. Red and beige box contains sixteen colored drawing crayons. 3¾in x 2¾in x ¾in (10cm x 7cm x 2cm). | $10-$15 |
| Crayolet Colored Drawing Crayons | Binney & Smith | 1940-1950s | No. 14. Red and beige box contains eight colored drawing crayons. 3¾in x 2¾in x 3/8in (10cm x 7cm x .9cm). | $10-$15 |
| Easy-Off Crayons | Binney & Smith | 1950s | No. 30. Red and white box contains twelve non-toxic crayons. 3¾in x 4¼in x 3/8in (10cm x 11cm x .9cm). | $5-$10 |
| Easy-Off Crayons | Binney & Smith | 1950s | No. 41. Red and white box contains eight non-toxic crayons. 3¾in x 2¾in x 3/8in (10cm x 7cm x .9cm). | $5-$10 |
| Perma Gold Medal Pressed Crayons | Binney & Smith | 1953 | No. 93. Navy and yellow box contains pressed crayons in eight colors. Lines on back for name, grade and school. "Ideal for line and mass drawing – Will not rub off or soil hands." 3¾in x 2¾in x 3/8in (10cm x 7cm x .9cm). | $10-$15 |
| Perma Pressed Crayon Sixteen Colors | Binney & Smith | 1953 | No. 85. Navy blue and white box has lift-off lid with Gold Medal logo. Box contains sixteen Perma pressed crayons. 4in x 5½in x ½in (10cm x 14cm x 1cm). | $10-$15 |
| Perma Pressed Crayon | Binney & Smith | circa 1957 | No. 85. Navy and yellow box has lift-off lid with Gold Medal logo. Box contains sixteen "versatile" Perma pressed crayons. 4in x 5½in x ½in (10cm x 14cm x 1cm). | $10-$15 |
| Perma Crayons | Binney & Smith | circa 1957 | No. 93. Navy and yellow box contains eight different brilliant colors. Non-toxic. "Versatile Crayons – For artwork, for maps, for charts and graphs" on back. 3¾in x 2¾in x 3/8in (10cm x 7cm x .9cm). | $10-$15 |

| ITEM | MANUFACTURER | YEAR | DESCRIPTION | ESTIMATED VALUE |
|---|---|---|---|---|
| Perma Crayons | Binney & Smith | circa 1957 | No. 9336. Navy and yellow box includes one dozen bulk (orange) crayons. Non-toxic. 3¾in x 2¼in x ¾in (10cm x 6cm x 2cm). | $10-$20 |
| Besco Large Anti-Roll® Pressed Crayons | Binney & Smith | 1959 | No. 1112. Navy and yellow box contains 12 Anti-Roll® pressed crayons. Non-toxic. ("Bulk" and color are stamped on box.) 4¼in x 1¾in x 1½in (11cm x 5cm x 4cm). | $10-$20 |
| Crayolet Assorted Colors Crayons | Binney & Smith | circa 1959 | No. 14. Red, yellow, black and white box contains eight assorted colors. Non-toxic. 3¾in x 2¾in x 3/8in (10cm x 7cm x .9cm). | $5-$15 |
| Crayolet Assorted Colors Crayons | Binney & Smith | 1960s | No. 14. Red, yellow, black and white box contains six assorted colors. Price: 5 cents. Non-toxic. 3¾in x 2in x 3/8in (10cm x 5cm x .9cm). | $5-$15 |
| Besco Anti-Roll® Type Drawing Crayon | Binney & Smith | 1960 | No. 10-B. Navy and beige box has lift-off lid with Gold Medal. Box contains eight large Anti-Roll® "kindergarten" crayons. 4½in x 4½in x ½in (12cm x 12cm x 1cm). | $10-$20 |
| Besco | Binney & Smith | circa 1960 | No. 1112. Black box with red label contains twelve large Anti-Roll® red crayons. (Bulk, stamped "RED.") 2¼in x 4½in x 1½in (6cm x 12cm x 4cm). | $15-$25 |
| Jumbo Washable Crayons | Binney & Smith | 1968 | No. 40. Red and white box contains eight jumbo size crayons. Box reads "The BIG crayon for little fingers." Price: 35 cents. 4½in x 3¾in x ½in (12cm x 10cm x 1cm). | $10-$20 |
| Non-Toxic Washable Crayons | Binney & Smith | 1968 | No. 60. Red and white box contains twelve colors. "Made by the Crayola® makers." Price: 19 cents. 4¼in x 4¾in x 3/8in (11cm x 12cm x .9cm). | $5-$15 |
| Besco Anti-Roll Drawing Crayons | Binney & Smith | circa 1975 | No. 10-BT. Navy and beige box contains eight large Anti-Roll® crayons. 4in x 4¼in x ½in (10cm x 11cm x 1cm). | $10-$20 |
| Artista II® Anti-Roll® Crayons | Binney & Smith | 1996 | No. 2108. White box has lift-off lid with red lettering and contains large Anti-Roll® crayons in different brilliant colors. Non-toxic. 4½in x 4½in x ½in (12cm x 12cm x 1cm). | $5-$15 |

### Molded Crayons

| ITEM | MANUFACTURER | YEAR | DESCRIPTION | ESTIMATED VALUE |
|---|---|---|---|---|
| Crayola® Gold Medal School Crayons | Binney & Smith | 1903 | No. 8. Original dark green and yellow box of eight colors – school crayons for educational color work. "Standard colors with brown and black." 3¾in x 2¾in x 3/8in (10cm x 7cm x .9cm). | $75-$125 |
| Crayola® Young Artists Drawing Crayons | Binney & Smith | 1904 | No. 51. Brown and gold box shows old-fashioned girl drawing on easel on front. Back lists names of the twenty-eight assorted colors. "These crayons will make clear, bright marks. Not injurious to the hands and will not soil the clothes. For coloring maps & pictures. Binney & Smith Co. New York-London-Paris-Hamburg." 7½in x 2½in x 3/8in (19cm x 6cm x .9cm). | $100-$125 |
| Crayola® Young Artists Drawing Crayons | Binney & Smith | circa 1904 | No. 57. Brown and gold box is a smaller version of No. 51 above. Back includes instructions for painting with crayons. Approximately 3½in x 4¼in x 3/8in (9cm x 11cm x .9cm). | $50-$75 |
| Crayola® Studio and School Crayons | Binney & Smith | Early 1900s | Old and unusual crayon box has "Crayola®" and "©" on the slide-off top. Includes eight colors and was manufactured expressly for the E.P. Charlton Stores (Massachusetts, Canada, Oregon and California). Approximately 4¼in x 2-7/8in x ½in (11cm x 7cm x 1cm). | $50-$75 |
| Crayola® Gold Medal School Crayons | Binney & Smith | circa 1910 | No. 16. (Original design) Dark green and yellow box of sixteen colors – school crayons for educational color work. "Standard colors with brown and black and eight additional shades." 3¾in x 2¾in x ¾in (10cm x 7cm x 2cm). | $30-$40 |

| ITEM | MANUFACTURER | YEAR | DESCRIPTION | ESTIMATED VALUE |
|---|---|---|---|---|
| Crayola® Gold Medal School Crayons | Binney & Smith | circa 1913 | No. 8. Dark green and yellow box of eight colors · school crayons for educational color work. 3¾in x 2¾in x 3/8in (10cm x 7cm x .9cm). | $20-$30 |
| Crayola® Gold Medal School Crayons | Binney & Smith | circa 1913 | No. 16. Dark green and yellow box of sixteen colors – school crayons for educational color work. "Spectrum colors with brown and black and eight additional hues." 3¾in x 2¾in x ¾in (10cm x 7cm x 2cm). | $20-$30 |
| "Rubens" Crayola® Artists' Crayon | Binney & Smith | circa 1913 | No. 24. Brown and beige box has picture of Rubens facing right and contains twenty-four artists' crayons. "The colors are equal to those used in the best artists' tube colors and pastels." 3¾in x 2¼in x 1½in (10cm x 6cm x 4cm). | $20-$30 |
| Rubens Crayola® Drawing Crayon | Binney & Smith | circa 1913-1920s | No. 24. Brown and beige box has lift-off top and picture of Rubens facing left. Contains twenty-four bright permanent colors. Back reads "The only crayon which artists consider a substitute for oil & water colors & pastels." 3¾in x 2¼in x 1½in (10cm x 6cm x 4cm). | $20-$30 |
| Rubens Crayola® | Binney & Smith | circa 1920s | No. 12. Brown and beige box contains twelve crayons such as "Egypt Olive Green" and "Philistines Burnt Sienna." Box was made especially for Littlefield Old Testament History Maps (The New York Sunday School Commission). 3¾in x 2in x ¾in (10cm x 5cm x 2cm). | $25-$35 |
| Crayola® Gold Medal School Crayons | Binney & Smith | 1919-1930s | No. 6. (Original design) Dark green and yellow box of six colors – school crayons for educational color work. "Standard colors." 3¾in x 2in x 3/8in (10cm x 5cm x .9cm). | $30-$40 |
| Crayola® Gold Medal School Crayons | Binney & Smith | 1920-1930s | No. 12. (Original design) Dark green and yellow box of school crayons for educational color work. "Twelve assorted colors including brown and black." 3¾in x 2in x ¾in (10cm x 5cm x 2cm). | $30-$40 |
| Crayola® Gold Medal School Crayons | Binney & Smith | circa 1920s | No. 6. Dark green and yellow box of six crayons – school crayons for educational color work. 3¾in x 2in x 3/8in (10cm x 5cm x .9cm). | $20-$30 |
| Crayola® Gold Medal School Crayons | Binney & Smith | circa 1920s | No. 12. Dark green and yellow box of twelve colors – school crayons for educational color work. 3¾in x 2in x ¾in (10cm x 5cm x 2cm). | $20-$30 |
| Munsell Crayola® Crayon | Binney & Smith | 1923-1943 | No. 12 M. Brown and beige box with lift-off top contains twelve colors. "Five principal hues and five intermediate hues at middle value and middle chroma – Five principal hues and five intermediate hues at maximum chroma with middle gray and black." 4in x 4in x ½in (10cm x 10cm x 1cm). | $20-$30 |
| Crayola® Gold Medal School Crayons | Binney & Smith | 1930s | No. 6. Dark green and yellow box includes six school crayons. "Good in any climate." 3¾in x 2in x 3/8in (10cm x 5cm x .9cm). | $15-$25 |
| Crayola® Gold Medal School Crayons | Binney & Smith | 1930s | No. 12. Dark green and yellow box includes twelve school crayons. "Good in any climate." Back reads "An Artist's Crayon at Scholar's Price. PERMANENT. WATERPROOF. Will not rub off." 3¾in x 2¾in x ¾in (10cm x 7cm x 2cm). | $15-$25 |
| Crayola® Gold Medal School Crayons | Binney & Smith | 1930s | No. 16. Dark green and yellow box includes sixteen school crayons. "Good in any climate." Back reads "An Artist's Crayon at Scholar's Price." Also includes lines for name, grade and school. 3¾in x 2¾in x ¾in (10cm x 7cm x 2cm). | $15-$25 |
| Crayola® Gold Medal School Crayons | Binney & Smith | 1933 | No. 8. Dark green and yellow box includes eight school crayons. "Good in any climate." Back has lines for name, grade and school. 3¾in x 2¾in x 3/8in (10cm x 7cm x .9cm). | $15-$20 |
| Crayola® Gold Medal School Crayons | Binney & Smith Canada Crayon Co. | circa 1933 | No. 8. Dark green and yellow box includes eight "colours." "Good in any climate." Back has lines for name, grade and school. 3¾in x 2¾in x 3/8in (10cm x 7cm x .9cm). | $20-$30 |

| ITEM | MANUFACTURER | YEAR | DESCRIPTION | ESTIMATED VALUE |
|---|---|---|---|---|
| Rubens Crayola® Gold Medal Drawing Crayon | Binney & Smith | 1940s | No. 38. Dark red and beige box with top that hinges on right side has eight colors. Gold Medal logo on label. 4½in x 3¾in x ½in (12cm x 10cm x 1cm). | $15-$20 |
| Crayola® Gold Medal School Crayons | Binney & Smith | 1940s | No. 16. Dark green and yellow box includes sixteen school crayons. "Good in any climate. Made in fifty colors." Back has lines for name, grade and school. 3¾in x 2¾in x ¾in (10cm x 7cm x 2cm). | $10-$15 |
| Crayola® Gold Medal Drawing Crayon | Binney & Smith | 1940s | No. 38. Gold and navy framed box with top that hinges on the right has eight colors. Crayons are six-sided. Gold Medal logo on label. 4½in x 3¾in x ½in (12cm x 10cm x 1cm). | $15-$20 |
| Rubens Crayola® Drawing Crayon | Binney & Smith | 1940-1950s | No. 241. Dark red and beige box has lift-off top and Gold Medal logo on label. Box contains twenty-four colors. 4in x 8in x ½in (10cm x 20cm x 1cm). | $15-$25 |
| Crayola® Gold Medal School Crayons | Binney & Smith | 1947 | No. 8. Dark blue-green and beige box contains eight school crayons. Back has lines for name, grade and school. 3¾in x 2¾in x 3/8in (10cm x 7cm x .9cm). | $15-$25 |
| Crayola® Gold Medal School Crayons | Binney & Smith | 1948 | No. 8. Dark green and yellow box includes eight school crayons. Back has lines for name, grade and school. 3¾in x 2¾in x 3/8in (10cm x 7cm x .9cm). | $10-$15 |
| Crayola® Crayons Winfield, Kansas | Binney & Smith | 1952 | No. 8. Dark green and yellow box commemorates opening of the Winfield Binney & Smith plant. Back reads "Compliments of Binney & Smith Winfield, October 8, 1952." 3¾in x 2¾in x 3/8in (10cm x 7cm x .9cm). | $30-$50 |
| Crayola® School Crayons | Binney & Smith | circa 1953 | No. 16. Dark green and yellow box with Gold Medal contains sixteen colors. Back has lines for name, grade and school. 3¾in x 2¾in x ¾in (10cm x 7cm x 2cm). | $10-$20 |
| Crayola® Drawing Crayon | Binney & Smith | circa 1953 | No. 38. Dark green and yellow box with eight crayons has Gold Medal logo and lift-off top. 4½in x 3¾in x ½in (12cm x 10cm x 1cm). | $10-$15 |
| Crayola® Drawing Crayon | Binney & Smith | circa 1953 | No. 38. Dark green and yellow box with eight six-sided crayons has Gold Medal logo and lift-off top. 4½in x 3¾in x ½in (12cm x 10cm x 1cm). | $10-$20 |
| Crayola® Drawing Crayon | Binney & Smith | 1953 | No. 48. Dark green and yellow box has picture of Rubens and Gold Medal logo. Box contains forty-eight crayons. Directions for stenciling are on back. 5in x 3in x 2in (13cm x 8cm x 5cm). | $15-$20 |
| Crayola® Gold Medal School Crayons | Binney & Smith | 1953 | No. 836. Beige box has bluish-green elf logo and lettering. Gold Medal logo. Thirty-six Crayola® school crayon sticks are red (bulk). 4in x 3¼in x 1¼in (10cm x 8cm x 3cm). | $15-$20 |
| Crayola® Drawing Crayon | Binney & Smith | 1953 | No. 24. Dark green and yellow box has Rubens Twenty-Four Colors with picture of Rubens and Gold Medal on front of box. Back has directions for stenciling. 4¾in x 2in x 1½in (12cm x 5cm x 4cm). | $15-$20 |
| Case of Rubens Crayola® Gold Medal Drawing Crayons | Binney & Smith | circa 1953 | Case contains a dozen boxes of No. 24 Rubens Crayola® Drawing Crayons for schoolroom use. Box has other Binney & Smith products listed. | $100 |
| Crayola® Gold Medal School Crayons | Binney & Smith | 1958 | No. 6. Dark green and yellow box includes six brilliant colors. "Good in any climate." Price: 10 cents. 3¾in x 2in x 3/8in (10cm x 5cm x .9cm). | $10-$20 |
| Crayola® Gold Medal School Crayons | Binney & Smith | 1958 | No. 8. Dark green and yellow box includes eight brilliant colors. "Good in any climate." Price: 15 cents. Lines on back for student to write name, grade and school. 3¾in x 2¾in x 3/8in (10cm x 7cm x .9cm). | $10-$15 |
| 64 Crayola® Crayons | Binney & Smith | 1958 | No. 64. Dark green and yellow original box has sixty-four different brilliant colors and built-in sharpener. Non-toxic. 5¼in x 5¾in x 1½in (13cm x 15cm x 4cm). | $25-$50 |

| ITEM | MANUFACTURER | YEAR | DESCRIPTION | ESTIMATED VALUE |
|---|---|---|---|---|
| Crayola® Crayons | Binney & Smith | circa 1958 | No. 8. Dark green and yellow box contains eight brilliant colors. Non-toxic. Price: 15 cents. Lines on back for name, grade and school. 3¾in x 2¾in x 3/8in (10cm x 7cm x .9cm). | $10-$15 |
| 8 Jumbo Crayola® Crayons | Binney & Smith | circa 1958 | No. 80. Dark green and yellow box contains eight jumbo crayons – "The BIG crayon for little fingers." Non-toxic. 4½in x 3¾in x ½in (12cm x 10cm x 1cm). | $10-$20 |
| 72 Crayons with Book of Crayon Projects | Binney & Smith | 1959 | No. 72. Large coloring set with cut out top (to show crayons inside) is dark gold and has picture of little boy with his dog. Box includes seventy-two crayons and sharpener. 14¾in x 7¾in x 1¼in (36cm x 20cm x 3cm). | $15-$30 |
| 48 Crayola® Crayons Different Brilliant Colors | Binney & Smith | circa 1960 | No. 48. Dark green and yellow box contains forty-eight different brilliant colors. Price: 89 cents. 5in x 3in x 2in (13cm x 8cm x 5cm). | $15-$20 |
| 48 Crayola® Crayons Canister | Binney & Smith | 1960s | No. 480. Dark green and yellow round twist-off canister with metal top contains forty-eight crayons. Price: 89 cents. Height is 4in (10cm). | $30-$50 |
| 8 Large Crayola® Crayons | Binney & Smith | circa 1962 | No. 38. Dark green and yellow box with lift-off lid contains eight large crayons. Non-toxic. 4½in x 3¾in x ½in (12cm x 10cm x 1cm). | $10-$15 |
| 12 Large Crayola® Crayons | Binney & Smith | circa 1962 | No. 33. Dark green and yellow box with lift-off lid contains twelve large yellow crayons. Non-toxic. 5¾in x 4½in x ½in (15cm x 12cm x 1cm). | $10-$20 |
| 8 Crayola® Crayons | Binney & Smith | 1963 | No. 8. Dark green and yellow box contains eight different brilliant colors. Crayon in Binney & Smith logo. Non-toxic. Back has lines for name, grade and school. 3¾in x 2¾in x 3/8in (10cm x 7cm x .9cm). | $5-$15 |
| 16 Crayola® Crayons | Binney & Smith | circa 1964 | No. 161. Dark green and yellow box contains sixteen different brilliant colors. Lift-off top. Non-toxic. Price: 30 cents. 3¾in x 5¾in x ½in (10cm x 15cm x 1cm). | $10-$20 |
| 16 Large Crayola® Crayons | Binney & Smith | circa 1965 | No. 336-A. Dark green and yellow box with lift-off lid contains sixteen large crayons in different brilliant colors. No wrappers. Non-toxic. 7¼in x 4½in x ¾in (19cm x 12cm x 2cm). | $10-$20 |
| 16 Crayola® Crayons | Binney & Smith | 1968 | No. 16-P. Dark green and yellow box in "New Plastic Container." Contains sixteen Different Brilliant Colors. Non-toxic. 4in x 3in x ¾in (10cm x 8cm x 2cm). | $10-$20 |
| 48 Crayola® Crayons Different Brilliant Colors | Binney & Smith | 1968 | No. 48. Dark green and yellow box contains forty-eight crayons and has newer Binney & Smith logo. Non-toxic. 5in x 3in x 2in (13cm x 8cm x 5cm). | $10-$20 |
| 72 Crayola® Crayons Drawing Set | Binney & Smith | 1968 | No. 72. Large coloring set with picture of boy and girl drawing, includes seventy-three crayons in crayon trays, round cardboard sharpener and two booklets: Crayola® Crayon Project Book and Creative Drawing Book. 14¾in x 7¾in x 1¼in (38cm x 20cm x 3cm). | $25-$50 |
| Large Crayola® Crayons | Binney & Smith | 1970s | No. 38. Dark green and yellow box with eight different brilliant colors has Gold Medal logo and lift-off top. Non-toxic. 4½in x 3¾in x ½in (12cm x 10cm x 1cm). | $10-$20 |
| 12 Crayola® Crayons | Binney & Smith | 1970s | No. 12. Dark green and yellow box contains twelve different brilliant colors. Non-toxic. 3¾in x 4¼in x ½in (10cm x 11cm x 1cm). | $10-$15 |
| Crayola® Fabric Colors | Binney & Smith | 1985 | Dark green and yellow box contains eight fabric crayons. (Zigzag "fabric" with pastel colors on label.) "For colorful designs on fabric." 3¾in x 2¾in x 3/8in (10cm x 7cm x .9cm). | $5-$15 |
| Crayola® Imagination Station Crayons | Binney & Smith Hallmark | 1987 | Dark green and yellow box contains twenty-four crayons with six metallic colors. Hallmark Stores exclusive. 3¾in x 2¾in x 1in (10cm x 7cm x 3cm). | $10-$20 |

| ITEM | MANUFACTURER | YEAR | DESCRIPTION | ESTIMATED VALUE |
|---|---|---|---|---|
| Crayola® Crayons 8 | Binney & Smith | 1988 | No. 8. Dark green and yellow box features open "smile" design for easy view of Crayola® crayons. ("Smile" was first used in 1988 package design.) 3¾in x 2¾in x 3/8in (10cm x 7cm x .9cm). | $5-$10 |
| Crayola® Crayons – FORD | Binney & Smith | 1988 | No. 52-0008. Dark green and yellow box contains eight different brilliant colors. 3¾in x 2¾in x 3/8in (10cm x 7cm x .9cm). | $10-$20 |
| 24 Crayola® Crayons | Binney & Smith Ontario | circa 1990 | No. 24. Dark green and yellow box contains twenty-four crayons. In English and French. Back has hand drawing of a leaf. 3¾in x 2¾in x 1in (10cm x 7cm x 3cm). | $10-$15 |
| 72 Crayola® Crayons | Binney & Smith | circa 1990 | Blue plastic carrying case with handle holds seventy-two crayons. 9¼in x 7in x 2in (24cm x 18cm x 5cm). | $10-$20 |
| 8 Crayola® Bunny Pastel Crayons | Binney & Smith | 1990 | Pastel box features open "smile" design and picture of Painter Bunny. Box contains eight pastel crayons. Price: $1.00. Approximately 3¾in x 2¾in x 3/8in (10cm x 7cm x .9cm). | $10-$15 |
| 16 Crayola® Bunny Crayons | Binney & Smith | 1990 | Pastel box features open "smile" design and picture of Painter Bunny. Box contains sixteen crayons. Price: $2.10. Approximately 3¾in x 2¾in x ¾in (10cm x 7cm x 2cm). | $10-$15 |
| Crayola® Pastel Crayons | Binney & Smith | 1990 | Dark green and yellow box has eight soft light colors. Back has Pink "Tip" with "Funky Flowers." 3¾in x 2¾in x 3/8in (10cm x 7cm x .9cm). | $5-$10 |
| Crayola® Crayons | Binney & Smith | 1990 | Dark green and yellow box has eight crayons. Back has Blue "Tip" and "lesson" – Scribble Surprises. Non-toxic. 3¾in x 2¾in x 3/8in (10cm x 7cm x .9cm). | $5-$10 |
| 24 Crayola® Crayons | Binney & Smith | 1990 | Dark green and yellow box contains twenty-four different brilliant colors. Blue "Tip" with "lesson" about circles and dots. Non-toxic. 3¾in x 2¾in x 1in (10cm x 7cm x 3cm). | $5-$10 |
| 64 Crayola® Crayons | Binney & Smith | 1990 | Dark green and yellow box has sixty-four crayons with built-in sharpener. Blue "Tip" with crayon stencil "lesson" on back. Non-toxic. 5¼in x 5¾in x 1½in (13cm x 15cm x 4cm). | $10-$15 |
| 16 Crayola® Crayons | Binney & Smith | 1990 | Dark green and yellow box contains sixteen different brilliant colors. Blue "Tip" has "lesson" on back – "Be in the Picture." 3¾in x 2¾in x ¾in (10cm x 7cm x 2cm). | $5-$10 |
| Crayola® Burger King Kids' Club Crayons | Burger King Binney & Smith | 1991 | Box contains three Fluorescent crayons and three Silver Swirl crayons. These crayons were given away at Burger King restaurants as part of the Kids' Club Worldwide Treasure Hunt promotion. Approximately 3¾in x 2¼in x 3/8in (10cm x 6cm x .9cm). | $10-$15 |
| Crayola® Colour 'n Smell Crayons | Binney & Smith Canada | circa 1992 | Dark green, yellow and purple box has eight crayons. "'Colour' to release the scent!" 3¾in x 2¾in x 3/8in (10cm x 7cm x .9cm). | $15-$20 |
| Winfield, Kansas 40th Birthday Crayola® Crayons | Binney & Smith | 1992 | No. 8. Dark green and yellow box commemorates the 40th Anniversary of the Winfield Binney & Smith plant. Back reads "Binney & Smith Winfield, 1952 – 1992, 40 Years Of Color In Kansas." Replica of the original 1952 box made in Winfield. 3¾in x 2¾in x 3/8in (10cm x 7cm x .9cm). | $25-$50 |
| Crayola® Crayons | Binney & Smith | 1992 | Dark green and yellow box contains four crayons. 3¾in x 1½in x 3/8in (10cm x 4cm x .9cm). | $5-$10 |
| Crayola® "Lavable Abwaschbar" | Binney & Smith Europe | 1994 | No. 878. Dark green and yellow box has colorful crayons on the front. Contains eight large washable crayons. Back shows pictures of fruit bowl and rainbow drawn with crayons. 5¾in x 5in x ½in (15cm x 13cm x 4cm). | $10-$20 |

137

| ITEM | MANUFACTURER | YEAR | DESCRIPTION | ESTIMATED VALUE |
|------|-------------|------|-------------|-----------------|
| 64 Crayola® Crayons | Binney & Smith Ontario | circa 1995 | No. 64. Dark green and yellow box has sixty-four different "colours" and built-in sharpener. Front has picture of airplane and Honda Odessey – grand prizes in Big Kid Classic Contest. In English and French. 6in x 5¾in x 1½in (15cm x 15cm x 4cm). | $10-$20 |
| Mickey's Stuff for Kids 16 Crayons – Crayola® | Disney Binney & Smith Canada | 1995 | Red box with cutout star features Mickey Mouse and contains sixteen octagonal no-roll crayons. Approximately 3¾in x 2¾in x 3/8in (10cm x 7cm x .9cm). | $15-$25 |
| Pooh Washable Crayons – Crayola® | Disney Binney & Smith Canada | 1995 | Pastel and white box features Winnie the Pooh and contains eight octagonal no-roll crayons. Approximately 4½in x 3¾in x ½in (12cm x 10cm x 1cm). | $15-$25 |
| Crayola® Flat Tops | Binney & Smith Distributed in Australia | 1995 | Green and yellow box shows a bird with a "flat top" holding a red crayon. Box contains eight no-roll crayons. "They rock but they don't roll." Approximately 4½in x 3¾in x ½in (12cm x 10cm x 1cm). | $10-$20 |
| Crayola® Colors Gift Set | Binney & Smith | 1996 | Dark green and yellow box with colorful pictures of forty-eight crayons, six markers, two ministampers and four colored pencils. Inside cover has picture of The Crayola FACTORY® and of each box in the set. Back gives additional information about The Crayola FACTORY® (includes coupon) and Crayola® trivia. 13¾in x 5¾in x 3/4in (35cm x 15cm x 2cm). | $15-$20 |
| "The Colours of Bermuda" | Binney & Smith | 1997 | "The Colours of Bermuda" box contains four "colours" – Dandelion, Sea Green, Periwinkle and Carnation Pink. 3¾in x 1½in x 3/8in (10cm x 4cm x .9cm). | $10-$15 |
| Crayola® Crayons True Blue Hero | Binney & Smith | 1997 | Small wooden slide box with dark blue lettering contains red lining holding a large "True Blue Hero" crayon. Approximately 6½in x 2½in x 1½in (117cm x 6cm x 4cm). | $5-$10 |
| Crayola® Kid's First Washable Crayons Classic Color | Binney & Smith | 1997 | Red, dark green and yellow box with colorful lettering, has eight jumbo crayons. For ages one to three. Certified non-toxic. 5¼in x 5in x ¾in (13cm x 13cm x 2cm). | $5-$10 |
| Crayola® Gold Medal – 1903 Replica | Binney & Smith | 1997 | No. 8. Dark green and yellow box contains eight crayons. Box is a replica of 1903 first box of Crayola® School Crayons. 3¾in x 2¾in x 3/8in (10cm x 7cm x .9cm). | $5-$10 |
| Crayola® Large Crayons 16 | Binney & Smith | 1997 | No. 52-0336. Dark green and yellow box with lift-off lid includes sixteen large crayons. 7¼in x 4½in x ¾in (19cm x 12cm x 2cm). | $10-$15 |
| Crayola® Holiday Crayons | Binney & Smith | 1997 | Dark green and yellow box has red and green "HOLIDAY" lettering on the front. Contains eight crayons, four glitter crayons, one each – Gold, Silver, Pine and Holiday Potpourri scented crayons. Non-toxic. 4¼in x 3¾in x ½in (11cm x 10cm x 1cm). | $5-$10 |
| Crayola® Crayons in Snuggle Soft Colors | Binney & Smith Lever Brothers | 1997 | Dark green and yellow box contains four pastel crayons with Snuggles on the label. "Ultra Snuggle with Color Protection." 3¾in x 1½in x 3/8in (10cm x 4cm x .9cm). | $5-$10 |
| Crayola® Crayons from your Friends at Hallmark | Hallmark Binney & Smith | 1997 | Dark green and yellow box contains four crayons. Clear label has Hallmark logo. 3¾in x 1½in x 3/8in (10cm x 4cm x .9cm). | $5-$10 |
| 64 Crayola® Crayons Featuring Built-in Sharpener | Binney & Smith | 1997 | Dark green and yellow box contains 64 crayons with built-in sharpener. Blue "Tip" advertises other Crayola® products on back. 5¼in x 5¾in x 1½in (13cm x 15cm x 4cm). | $10-$15 |
| 96 Crayola® Big Box of Crayons | Binney & Smith | 1997 | Dark green and yellow box with built-in sharpener has ninety-six crayons. Red "Tip" on front surrounded by Crayola® crayons. Certified non-toxic. Back has variety of other Crayola® products and place for name. 8½in x 5in x 1½in (22cm x 13cm x 4cm). | $10-$15 |

| ITEM | MANUFACTURER | YEAR | DESCRIPTION | ESTIMATED VALUE |
|------|--------------|------|-------------|-----------------|
| 96 Crayola® Crayons Big Box | Binney & Smith Ontario | 1997 | No. 96. Bright yellow Big Box (Grosse Boite) includes eight retro "colours" dedicated to eight Canadian Heroes. "They're groovy, they're hip, and now they're heroic!" Box has built-in sharpener. 5in x 5¾in x 2¼in (13cm x 15cm x 6cm). | $10-$20 |
| 112 Crayola® Crayons – The Ultimate Crayon Collection | Binney & Smith | 1997 | Dark green and yellow "cigar-type box" has coloring book on top with "outside the lines." Inside are two boxes of forty-eight and a box of sixteen Crayola® crayons. 8¾in x 5½in x 2½in (22cm x 14cm x 6cm). | $10-$15 |
| Crayola® Canada Crayons | Binney & Smith Canada | circa 1998 | No. 82. Dark green and yellow box has Blue "Tip" and red Canadian maple leaf on label. In French and English. Contains eight crayons. "Favorite Colours Voted by Canadians!" 3¾in x 2¾in x 3/8in (10cm x 7cm x .9cm). | $10-$15 |
| Crayola® Canada Crayons | Binney & Smith Canada | circa 1998 | Dark green and yellow box has red Canadian maple leaf on label. In French and English. Contains eight crayons. "Favorite Colours Voted by Canadians!" 3¾in x 2¾in x 3/8in (10cm x 7cm x .9cm). | $10-$15 |
| 8 Crayola® Crayons Certified Non-Toxic | Binney & Smith | 1998 | Dark green and yellow box contains eight crayons. Box has cutout "smile design" to view Crayola® crayons. 3¾in x 2¾in x 3/8in (10cm x 7cm x .9cm). | $5-$10 |
| The Crayola FACTORY® Crayons | Hallmark Binney & Smith | 1998 | Dark green and yellow box contains four crayons from The Crayola FACTORY®. Gives information about factory tours. 3¾in x 1½in x 3/8in (10cm x 4cm x .9cm). | $5-$10 |
| Crayola® Crayons "Happy 40th Birthday" | Binney & Smith | 1998 | Limited Edition replica of 1958 box includes "64 Original Colors." Slide-on dark green cover includes "Free Gifts Inside." Back lists all sixty-four color names in original box of sixty-four Crayola® crayons. Includes built-in sharpener. 6in x 5¾in x 2in (15cm x 15cm x 5cm). | $10-$20 |
| Crayola® Crayon Canadian 1958 Box Replica | Binney & Smith Canada | 1998 | Limited Edition replica of 1958 box includes sixty-four original "colours" and built-in sharpener. Slide-on bright yellow cover with balloons. In English and French. Back reads "1958 North American Icon is Born." 5in x 5¾in x 1½in (13cm x 15cm x 4cm). | $10-$20 |
| Smucker's Toppings Crayola® "TechnoBrite" | Hallmark Binney & Smith | 1999 | Dark green, yellow and purple Sample Pack. Not for Resale. Contains six crayons. "TechnoBRITE" appears on the front of the box on a computer screen. Certified non-toxic. 3¾in x 2¼in x 3/8in (10cm x 6cm x .9cm). | $5-$15 |
| Construction Paper™ Crayola® Crayons | Hallmark Binney & Smith | 1999 | Dark green, yellow and purple Sample Pack. Not for Resale. Contains four certified non-toxic crayons. 3¾in x 1½in x 3/8in (10cm x 4cm x .9cm). | $5-$10 |
| 120 Crayola® Wizard's Giant Box of Crayons | Binney & Smith | 1999 | Bright yellow "cigar-type box" has 120 different crayons. Surprise inside is blue washable marker. Has picture of wizard, castle, dinosaur and red "Tip." Inside are two boxes of forty-eight and box of twenty-four non-toxic crayons. Back of box includes photographs and tells how crayons are made. 8¾in x 5½in x 2½in (22cm x 14cm x 6cm). | $10-$15 |
| Crayola® Metallic "Sampler Kit" | Energizer Binney & Smith | 2000 | Red plastic box with hanger has dark green and yellow label with picture of Energizer Bunny. Four metallic crayons, two metallic markers and Construction Paper pad. 5in x 5½in x 3/4in (13cm x 14cm x 2cm). | $10-$15 |
| Crayola® Crayons 12 | Hallmark Binney & Smith | 2000 | Dark green and yellow box contains twelve crayons. Back is ad for Crayola® Crayon Classpack®. Non-toxic. 3¾in x 4¼in x ½in (10cm x 11cm x 1cm). | $5-$10 |
| Crayola® Fabric Crayons | Hallmark Binney & Smith | 2000 | Dark green and yellow box contains eight fabric crayons. Fabric zigzag design on front of box. Non-toxic. 3¾in x 2¾in x 3/8 (10cm x 7cm x .9cm). | $5-$10 |

| ITEM | MANUFACTURER | YEAR | DESCRIPTION | ESTIMATED VALUE |
|---|---|---|---|---|
| Crayola® Kid's First® Washable Crayons | Hallmark Binney & Smith | 2000 | Dark green and yellow box includes eight large washable crayons. Back has "lesson" about drawing shapes. Non-toxic. 4¼in x 3¾in x ½in (11cm x 10cm x 1cm). | $5 |
| 8 Crayola® Multicultural Crayons | Hallmark Binney & Smith | 2000 | Dark green and yellow box of multicultural crayons has picture of children around the world. Non-toxic. 3¾in x 2¾in x ¾in (10cm x 7cm x 1cm). | $5 |
| 16 Crayola® Multicultural Crayons | Hallmark Binney & Smith | 2000 | Dark green and yellow box of multicultural crayons has picture of children around the world. Non-toxic. 3¾in x 2¾in x 3/8in (10cm x 7cm x .9cm). | $5-$10 |
| 24 Crayola® "Mes Debuts" | Binney & Smith France | circa 2000 | Round clear plastic box has dark green and yellow label in French. Contains twenty-four short "fat" crayons for children ages two and up. Height is 3in (8cm). | $10 |
| America's Favorite 50 Crayons | Binney & Smith | 2001 | Round clear container contains the top fifty favorite colors chosen by American consumers. Each Crayola® crayon has a special gold label that ranks its color's popularity. Approximately 4in (10cm). | $10 |
| Red, White and Blue Box of 64 | Binney & Smith | 2001 | Box of sixty-four contains all red, white and blue Crayola® crayons. Other color combinations are available from www.CrayolaStore.com. 5¼in x 5¾in x 1½in (13cm x 15cm x 4cm). | $10 |

## Category: DOLLS, ANIMALS and PLUSH TOYS

| ITEM | MANUFACTURER | YEAR | DESCRIPTION | ESTIMATED VALUE |
|---|---|---|---|---|
| Red Crayola® Bear | Hallmark Binney & Smith | 1986 | Furry red bear wears red "Crayola®" sweater. 14in (36cm). | $10-$20 |
| Orange Crayola® Bear | Hallmark Binney & Smith | 1986 | Furry orange bear wears orange "Crayola®" sweater. 14in (36cm). | $15-$25 |
| Yellow Crayola® Bear | Hallmark Binney & Smith | 1986 | Furry yellow bear wears yellow "Crayola®" sweater. 14in (36cm). | $10-$20 |
| Green Crayola® Bear | Hallmark Binney & Smith | 1986 | Furry green bear wears green "Crayola®" sweater. 14in (36cm). | $15-$25 |
| Blue Crayola® Bear (Medium) | Hallmark Binney & Smith | 1986 | Furry blue bear wears blue "Crayola®" sweater. 14in (36cm). | $10-$20 |
| Purple Crayola® Bear | Hallmark Binney & Smith | 1986 | Furry purple bear wears purple Crayola® sweater. 14in (36cm). | $10-$20 |
| Set of four Crayola® Bears (Small) Promotional Item | Burger King Binney & Smith | 1986 | Red, yellow, blue and purple bears wear matching "Crayola®" sweaters. 7in (18cm). | $15-$20 |
| Blue Crayola® Bear (Large) | Mervyn's Binney & Smith | circa 1986 | Furry blue bear wears blue "Crayola®" sweater. 21in (53cm). | $15-$25 |

Note: Other sizes of bears available at comparable prices; ORANGE and GREEN are the hardest to find and usually more valuable. (Measurements of all stuffed animals and toys are approximate.)

| ITEM | MANUFACTURER | YEAR | DESCRIPTION | ESTIMATED VALUE |
|---|---|---|---|---|
| Pink Crayola® Bunny | Hallmark Binney & Smith | 1988 | Soft pastel pink bunny wears pink "Crayola®" sweater. 12in (31cm). | $10-$20 |
| Yellow Crayola® Bunny | Hallmark Binney & Smith | 1988 | Soft pastel yellow bunny wears yellow "Crayola®" sweater. 8in (20cm). | $10-$15 |
| Crayola® Lavender Lou Bunny in Paint Can | Hallmark Binney & Smith | 1989 | Crayola® Lavender Lou bunny wears painter's cap and sits inside a paint can. 9in (23cm). | $10-$15 |
| Crayola® Circus Monkey | Hallmark Heartline | 1989 | Large yellow monkey has a Crayola® circus ribbon around his neck and yellow "crayon tip" hat. 24in (61cm). | $15-$25 |
| Crayola® Circus Dog | Hallmark Heartline | 1989 | Small red dog has a Crayola® circus ribbon around his neck and red "crayon tip" hat. 12in (31cm). | $10-$20 |

| ITEM | MANUFACTURER | YEAR | DESCRIPTION | ESTIMATED VALUE |
|---|---|---|---|---|
| Crayola® Circus Elephant | Hallmark Heartline | 1989 | Small blue elephant has a Crayola® circus ribbon around his neck and blue "crayon tip" hat. 12in (31cm). | $10-$20 |
| Crayola® Circus Horse | Hallmark Heartline | 1989 | Small purple horse has a Crayola® circus ribbon around his neck and blue "crayon tip" hat. 12in (31cm). | $10-$20 |
| Crayola® Circus Lion | Hallmark Heartline | 1989 | Large green lion was used as a Binney & Smith promotional item. 21in (53cm). | $15-$25 |
| Crayola® Painter Candy Cotton Tail | Hallmark Binney & Smith | 1990 | Crayola® pink girl bunny wears pink dress and panties and has aqua and white polka-dotted ribbon. 13in (33cm). | $15-$20 |
| Crayola® Painter Bunny | Hallmark Binney & Smith | 1990 | Crayola® white boy bunny wears aqua painter's cap and pink "paint spattered" overalls with yellow bandana around his neck. 13in (33cm). | $15-$20 |
| Daffadilly Duck | Hallmark Heartline | 1990 | Bright yellow girl duck wears pink "Crayola®" dress, ribbon in hair, and plastic legs and pink shoes. 11in (28cm). | $10-$15 |
| Squiggles | Hallmark Heartline | 1990 | Bright yellow boy duck with aqua shirt and sailor hat. Plastic legs with aqua tennis shoes. 9in (23cm). | $10-$15 |
| Crayola® Boy | Binney & Smith | circa 1990 | Light blue Crayola® boy holds a multicolored ball and wears pink tennis shoes. 7in (18cm). | $10-$15 |
| Crayola® Girl | Binney & Smith | circa 1990 | Hot pink Crayola® girl has yellow bow and aqua shoes. 7in (18cm). | $10-$15 |
| Crayola® Kids Crayon Boy | Binney & Smith | 1991 | Purple Crayola® Kids Boy doll wears an orange muscle shirt, headband and green and orange sneakers. Weighted bottom. Approximately 16in (41cm). | $10-$20 |
| Crayola® Kids Crayon Girl | Binney & Smith | 1991 | Turquoise Crayola® Kids Girl doll wears a multicolored skirt and vest and has a pink bow in hair, orange boots and glasses. Approximately 17in (43cm). | $10-$20 |
| Crayola® Kids Football Player | Commonwealth Toys Binney & Smith | 1991 | Neon green Crayola® plush football player has orange jersey #54, football and purple and white shoes with cleats. 16in (41cm). | $10-$20 |
| Crayola® Kids Cheerleader | Commonwealth Toys Binney & Smith | 1991 | Hot pink Crayola® plush cheerleader doll has pink and yellow outfit with "C" and saddle oxford shoes. 16in (41cm). | $10-$20 |
| Crayola® Ballerina Bear | Gund Binney & Smith | circa 1996 | White bear is dressed in dance tutu and ballet slippers. She has a "Crayola®" headpiece made up of five colorful crayons. 15in (38cm). | $15-$20 |
| Crayola® Bear with Beanie | Gund Binney & Smith | circa 1996 | Large brown bear wears multicolored beanie and red Crayola® shirt. The bottoms of his feet have Crayola® boxes on them. 12in (31cm). | $15-$20 |
| Crayola® Bear Rainbow Sweater (Large) | Gund Binney & Smith | circa 1996 | Large brown bear wears colorful striped sweater in rainbow colors. The bottoms of his feet have Crayola® boxes on them. 12in (31cm). | $15-$20 |
| Crayola® Bear Rainbow Sweater (Small) | Gund Binney & Smith | circa 1996 | Small brown bear wears colorful striped sweater in rainbow colors. The bottoms of his feet have Crayola® boxes on them. 9in (23cm). | $10-$15 |
| Crayola® Storybook Friends Bonnie and Lonnie | Hallmark Binney & Smith | 1997 | Boy and girl mice with aqua striped matching outfits. Lonnie holds a straw hat and Bonnie carries a straw basket. 10in (25cm). | $10-$20 |
| *Crayola® Green* Madame Alexander Doll | Madame Alexander Americana Collection | 1999 | **Caucasian Crayola® Green wears green flared-leg pants, midi top and green and black cap. She has blonde braids and blue eyes. 8in (20cm). | $50-$75 |
| *Crayola® Red* Madame Alexander Doll | Madame Alexander Americana Collection | 1999 | **Caucasian Crayola® Red wears a red skirt, bolero jacket and tam trimmed in black with colorful "hand" accents. She has black hair, eyes and freckles. 8in (20cm). | $50-$75 |

| ITEM | MANUFACTURER | YEAR | DESCRIPTION | ESTIMATED VALUE |
|------|--------------|------|-------------|-----------------|
| *Crayola®* Yellow Madame Alexander Doll | Madame Alexander Americana Collection | 1999 | **African-American Crayola® Yellow wears a yellow mini jumper with colorful button trim over black shirt and tights with a matching yellow wide-brimmed hat. She has black hair and brown eyes. 8in (20cm). | $50-$75 |
| *Crayola®* Blue Madame Alexander Doll | Madame Alexander Americana Collection | 1999 | **Caucasian Crayola® Blue wears a blue felt jumper with black trim and colorful ABC's and a matching blue spiked hat. She has blonde hair, blue eyes and freckles. 8in (20cm). | $50-$75 |
| *Crayola®* Megan Madame Alexander Doll | Madame Alexander Americana Collection | 1999 | **Caucasian Crayola® Megan wears an old-fashioned red and gold calico dress trimmed with green and gold plaid. An ivory piqué pinafore has two pockets with an early box of Crayola® crayons. She has brown hair and blue eyes and carries a mini drawing pad. 14in (36cm). | $65-$95 |

**Note: All Crayola® dolls from the Madame Alexander *Americana Collection* are available in Caucasian and African-American.

| ITEM | MANUFACTURER | YEAR | DESCRIPTION | ESTIMATED VALUE |
|------|--------------|------|-------------|-----------------|
| Crayola® "Tip" Key Chains | Binney & Smith | 1999 | Crayola® key chains available in red, blue and yellow "Tip" with hands, and legs which have tennis shoes that tie. 6½in (17cm). | $5 |
| Dale Whale Crayola® Key Chain | Binney & Smith | 1999 | Cloth fuchsia whale with black stripes has aqua fur spout. 4-3/8in (11cm). | $5 |
| Myrtle Sue Turtle Crayola® Key Chain | Binney & Smith | 1999 | Cloth blue and green turtle has yellow eyes. 4½in (12cm). | $5 |
| Pittypat Cat Crayola® Key Chain | Binney & Smith | 1999 | Cloth orange cat with black stripes has red patch over right eye. 3-3/8in (9cm). | $5 |
| Squirmy Wormy Crayola® Key Chain | Binney & Smith | 1999 | Cloth red worm with green fur on head has yellow eyes. 3-7/8in (10cm). | $5 |
| VeryShy Butterfly Crayola® Key Chain | Binney & Smith | 1999 | Cloth pink butterfly with purple wings has aqua antennae. 3-3/8in (9cm). | $5 |

Note: Several other animal key chains are available in this series.

| ITEM | MANUFACTURER | YEAR | DESCRIPTION | ESTIMATED VALUE |
|------|--------------|------|-------------|-----------------|
| Crayola® Blue "Tip" Plush | Binney & Smith | 2000 | Blue velour "Tip" has embroidered details in black with green and white vinyl shoes. 13in (33cm). | $15 |
| Crayola® Red "Tip" Plush | Binney & Smith | 2000 | Red velour "Tip" has embroidered details in black with yellow and white vinyl shoes. 13in (33cm). | $15 |
| Crayola® Yellow "Tip" Plush | Binney & Smith | 2000 | Yellow velour "Tip" has embroidered details in black with red and white vinyl shoes. 13in (33cm). | $15 |
| Crayola® Green "Tip" Plush | Binney & Smith | 2000 | Green velour "Tip" has embroidered details in black with blue and white vinyl shoes. 13in (33cm). | $15 |
| Crayola® Plush Toy Crayon | Hallmark Binney & Smith | 2000 | Stuffed terry cloth crayons available in red, blue and yellow with black Crayola® logo. 7¾in (20cm). | $5-$10 |
| Crayola® Kangaroo | Hallmark Binney & Smith | 2000 | Purple Crayola® kangaroo has red shirt, lime green pouch and aqua trim on ears and feet. 12in (31cm). | $15-$25 |
| Honey Bee Bear and Crayola® Set | Mary Kay Binney & Smith | 2000 | Light brown bear is dressed in a bumblebee costume. Back has a zipper pouch that holds a Crayola® doodling pad, activity book and markers. 12in (31cm). | $15-$25 |

# Category: LUNCHBOXES, PENCIL BOXES and OTHER CONTAINERS

| ITEM | MANUFACTURER | YEAR | DESCRIPTION | ESTIMATED VALUE |
|------|--------------|------|-------------|-----------------|
| Crayola® CLAY TIME® Container featuring Jim Henson's Muppets Container | Binney & Smith | 1982 | Bright yellow plastic container with green "crayon tip" lid and handle has likeness of Gonzo, Fozzie and Kermit. 10in (25cm). | $10-$20 |
| THE Crayola® BOX | Binney & Smith | 1982 | Crayola® storage box is available in red, green, blue and yellow and includes sixteen crayons, chalk, markers and sharpener. 6in x 8½in x 1½in (15cm x 22cm x 4cm). | $15-$20 |

| ITEM | MANUFACTURER | YEAR | DESCRIPTION | ESTIMATED VALUE |
|---|---|---|---|---|
| Old Wooden "Crayola" Box | Unknown | n.d. | Dark green and brown box has crude "Crayola" printed on top. Made to look old. Top is hinged with leather ties. 4¼in x 7½in (11cm x 19cm). | $15-$25 |
| Glass Canister with "Crayola" Etching | Unknown | n.d. | Clear glass canister has "Crayola" etched in cursive. Height is approximately 4in (10cm). | $10-$20 |
| Crayola® Plastic Watch Box | Binney & Smith | circa 1984 | White plastic box has picture of Crayola® box on lift-off lid. "The Original Crayola® Armitron Collectibles." Approximately 2½in x 5¾in x ¾in (6cm x 15cm x 2cm). | $3-$5 |
| Crayola® Crayon Bank | Binney & Smith | circa 1987 | Yellow Crayola® crayon is a bank. Height is approximately 9½in (24cm). | $10-$15 |
| Crayola® So Big® Bucket | Binney & Smith | 1989 circa | Large yellow crayon-shaped bucket with green handle features "Tip" and Crayola® crayons and contains "So Big®" crayons. Approximate height is 8in (20cm). | $10-$20 |
| Crayola® Crayon Bank | Ralphco, Inc. Binney & Smith | 1980-1990s | Purple crayon-shaped bank has clear middle section to view coins. Height is 11¾in (30cm). | $10-$15 |
| Crayola® Pencil Box | Creative Plastics Binney & Smith | circa 1990s | Lunchbox-style red plastic pencil box has handle that snaps closed. Paper label includes picture of eight crayons. Also available in blue. 5in x 8in x 2½in (13cm x 20cm x 6cm). | $5-$10 |
| Crayola® Pencil Box | Creative Plastics Binney & Smith | circa 1990s | Lunchbox-style red plastic pencil box has handle that snaps closed. Paper label includes child-like drawing of school bus. 5in x 8in x 2½in (13cm x 20cm x 6cm). | $5-$10 |
| Crayola® Pencil Box | Creative Plastics Binney & Smith | circa 1990s | Lunchbox-style blue plastic pencil box has handle that snaps closed. Paper label includes child-like drawing of the alphabet. 5in x 8in x 2½in (13cm x 20cm x 6cm). | $5-$10 |
| Crayola® Crayon Pencil Box with Calculator | Advanced Concepts Binney & Smith | circa 1990s | Red plastic crayon-shaped pencil box includes a calculator inside. Approximately 8½in (22cm). | $10-$15 |
| Plastic Lunchbox and Thermos | Thermos Binney & Smith | 1991 | Purple lunchbox has picture of Crayola® box with five crayons. Includes white thermos with purple top and colorful crayons. 7¼in x 8¾in x 4in (19cm x 22cm x 10cm). | $10-$20 |
| Vinyl Lunchbox with Thermos | Thermos Binney & Smith | 1991 | Black vinyl lunchbox has red, yellow and blue checks with picture of boy skateboarding on a Crayola® crayon. Includes white thermos with red top and colorful crayons. 7¾in x 10in x 3¾in (20cm x 25cm x 10cm). | $15-$20 |
| Crayola® Gold Medal Colors Pencil Box | Binney & Smith | 1993 | Red and yellow pencil box has back hinge that opens like a cigar box. Includes old "Crayola®" trademark and graphics. 5¼in x 8in x 2¼in (13cm x 20cm x 6cm). | $15-$40 |
| Crayola® Plastic Watch Crayon Box | Binney & Smith | 1994 | Red plastic crayon-shaped box has clear section to show watch. Height is 5-3/8in (14cm). | $3-$5 |
| Crayon-Shaped Cheerios Box | General Mills Binney & Smith | 1994 | Crayon-shaped container was made in several colors with the familiar yellow Cheerios logo. Cereal box contains three Crayola® crayons. Height 12in (31cm). | $10-$15 |
| Crayola® Time Capsule | Binney & Smith | circa 2000 | Green crayon-shaped time capsule contains Model Magic® and Crayola® markers. Height is 12in (31cm). | $10-$15 |
| Canadian Crayola® "Tip" | Binney & Smith Canada | circa 2001 | Red plastic container is "Tip" filled with crayons, markers and other fun items. Box is printed in French. Approximate height is 12½in (32cm). | $20-$25 |
| Crayola® Creative Garden | Binney & Smith | circa 2001 | Round white plastic garden dish includes plant identification stake. 4¾in (12cm). | $5-$10 |
| "Lots-A-Paint" Can | Binney & Smith | 2001 | Looks like an actual can of house paint. Includes a variety of Crayola® paints, brushes and projects. Height is approximately 7½in (19cm). | $15-$20 |

# Category: MEMORABILIA and COLLECTIBLES

**Crayola® Color and Paint Sets**
**"Crayola®" Toy Sets and Games**

| ITEM | MANUFACTURER | YEAR | DESCRIPTION | ESTIMATED VALUE |
|---|---|---|---|---|
| "Art-Toy" Set | Binney & Smith | Early 1900s | Art set has picture of girl and boy working at table. "Now Any Child Can Transfer Many Wonderful Pictures." | $50-$75 |
| Crayola® Little Folks Outfit | Binney & Smith | 1920s | No. 25. Set includes twelve assorted Crayola® crayons (3¼in [9cm]), stencils and drawing book and paper. Color graphics of Dutch boy chasing geese on hinged front cover. (Also available with lift-off top.) | $30-$50 |
| Crayola® Little Folks Outfit | Binney & Smith | 1920s | No. 50. Set includes twelve assorted Crayola® crayons (6in [15cm]), stencils and drawing book and paper. Color graphics of Dutch girl and windmill on hinged front cover. (Also available with lift-off top.) Earlier version named "Crayola®" Kindergarten Outfit. | $30-$50 |
| Crayola® Picture Tracer Outfit | Binney & Smith | 1920s | No. 75. Set includes seventeen assorted Rubens Crayola® crayons, black outline crayon, metal tracer, colored pictures and roll of tracing paper. Color graphics of Little Red Riding Hood inside. Hinged front cover shows children drawing. (Also available with lift-off top.) | $50-$100 |
| Crayola® Snowbound Color Box | Binney & Smith | 1920s | No. 500. Set includes four assorted Crayola® crayons, drawing book, water colors and quill brush. Lift-off cover has color graphics of children drawing inside the house during snowstorm. | $30-$50 |
| "Little Boy Blue" Paint Box | Binney & Smith | 1920s | No. 501. Set contains fourteen assorted water colors, mixing pan and quill brush. Lift-off cover has color graphics of Little Boy Blue under the haystack. (Earlier version has boy sitting on fence playing horn.) | $50-$75 |
| Crayola® Trace It and Paint It Outfit | Binney & Smith | 1920s | No. 502. Set contains five assorted Crayola® crayons, water color cakes, mixing pan, camel's hair brush, tracing pad, stencils and outline drawings with stories. Lift-off cover has color graphics of boy, girl with toys and dog in classroom. (Earlier version has boy and girl drawing at a table.) | $50-$75 |
| Crayola® Home Run Color Box | Binney & Smith | circa 1920s | No. 503. Set contains five "Crayola®" crayons, water colors, mixing pans and brush. Lift-off cover has color graphics of baseball players. | $30-$50 |
| Crayola® Crusader Color Box | Binney & Smith | 1920s | No. 503. Set includes four assorted Crayola® crayons, water colors, mixing pan and quill brush. Lift-off cover has color graphics of crusader on horse. | $30-$50 |
| Uncle Wiggily "Crayola®" Color Box | Binney & Smith | 1920s | No. 506. Set includes eight assorted crayons, stencils, drawing book and paper. Color graphics of Uncle Wiggily on hinged front cover. | $50-$75 |
| "Uncle Wiggily" Water Color Box | Binney & Smith | 1920s | No. 507. Set contains sixteen pans of water color paints and camel's hair brush. Metal box has five-color lithograph of Uncle Wiggily. | $50-$100 |
| Crayola® Color Kit for Kiddies | Binney & Smith | 1920s | No. 508. Set includes four assorted Crayola® crayons, water color cakes, mixing pan, camel's hair brush and six outline drawings with stories. Lift-off cover has color graphics of lady on staircase and children drawing. | $30-$50 |
| Crayola® Little Women Color and Sewing Box | Binney & Smith | circa 1920s | No. 509. Blue box contains eight Crayola® crayons, artists' sketching crayons, pencils, water colors, tubes of moist paint, mixing pan, brush, soap eraser, ruler, thread, needles, doll's semi-made dress, scissors, thimble, box of chalk and Pleasant Pastime Crayon Book. | $50-$100 |
| Crayola® Chummy Animals Color Set | Binney & Smith | 1920s | No. 510. Set includes six assorted Crayola® crayons, drawing book, water colors, mixing pan and camel's hair brush. Lift-off cover has color graphics of dressed up animal friends. | $30-$50 |

| ITEM | MANUFACTURER | YEAR | DESCRIPTION | ESTIMATED VALUE |
|---|---|---|---|---|
| Crayola® Rob Roy Color Box | Binney & Smith | 1920s | No. 513. Set includes ten assorted Crayola® crayons, water colors, mixing pans and camel's hair brush. Lift-off cover has a picture of Rob Roy in kilt playing bagpipes. | $30-$50 |
| Crayola® Bird-Land Color Set | Binney & Smith | 1920s | No. 516. Set includes six assorted Crayola® crayons, water color cakes, mixing pan, camel's hair brush and packet of bird stories to color. Lift-off cover has color graphics of two birds. | $30-$50 |
| Crayola® Young Artists' Set | Binney & Smith | circa 1920s | No. 517. Set includes nine water colors, eight Crayola® sketching crayons, pencil, mixing pans, brush and Toyland Painting Book. | $30-$50 |
| Crayola® Dream Stories Color Set | Binney & Smith | 1920s | No. 517. Set includes five assorted Crayola® crayons, water color cakes, mixing pans, camel's hair brush and packet of dream stories to color. Lift-off cover has color graphics of prince and princess. | $30-$50 |
| Crayola® Gift Box | Binney & Smith | 1920s | No. 518. Box includes six Crayola® crayons, water colors, tubes of color, brush, penholder and pen, pencil, mixing pans and six Grace G. Drayton drawings to color. "Packed in a substantial wooden frame, cardboard box with brass clasps." | $50-$100 |
| Crayola® Golden Treasure Color Set | Binney & Smith | 1920s | No. 518. Set includes ten assorted Crayola® crayons, drawing book, wooden cups with water colors, water color cakes, mixing pans, camel's hair brush and packet of stories to color. Lift-off cover has color graphics of king on his throne. | $50-$100 |
| Crayola® Color Wheel Game | Binney & Smith | 1981 | Drawing game for creating colorful pictures with stencils and Crayola® crayons. | $10-$20 |
| Crayola® Creative Lettering | Binney & Smith | 1989 | Crayola® markers and booklet for learning to write in beautiful calligraphy. | $10-$15 |
| Crayola® Colorable Playing Cards | Binney & Smith | 1997 | Fifty-two playing cards in dark green and yellow Crayola® box with drawings of spade, diamond, heart and club in different colors. Box of four crayons also included. Both boxes are inside a clear plastic velcro-closed bag. | $5 |

**Binney & Smith Memorabilia**

| ITEM | MANUFACTURER | YEAR | DESCRIPTION | ESTIMATED VALUE |
|---|---|---|---|---|
| Authentic Crayola® Factory Stock Box | Binney & Smith | 1903-1996 | Large wooden crate was used to sort crayons in factory. Includes "Certificate of Authenticity." Approximately 24in x 14in x 8½in (61cm x 36cm x 22cm). | $30-$45 |
| Old Binney & Smith Envelope | Binney & Smith | 1904 | Envelope with Binney & Smith return address says "Fine Lamp Blacks and Pure Carbons" and has two-cent cancelled stamp and 1904 postmark. | $15-$25 |
| "Defend America Coin Saving Book" | Binney & Smith | 1940s | Red, white, and blue book with patriotic theme has pictures of the Crayola® elves saving money. Made to encourage children to save coins to buy United States Defense Stamps and Bonds. Includes an introductory letter by the Binney & Smith Chairman of the Board. 8¾in x 7¾in (22cm x 20cm). | $50-$100 |
| Crayola® Wire Display Rack | Binney & Smith | circa 1958 | Wire rack with yellow and green "Crayola® Crayons" sign in store was used to display crayon boxes. Two screw clamps on back for attaching to shelf or ledge. 30in x 4in x 2½in (76cm x 10cm x 6cm). | $20-$30 |
| Crayola® Metal Display Rack | Binney & Smith | 1960 | Freestanding black metal rack with white "Visit the Crayola® Corner" and yellow and green "Crayola® Crayons from 15¢ to $1.00" sign used to display crayon boxes. Base is 16in x 16in (41cm x 4cm). Height is 21in (53cm) to the top of the sign and 10in (25cm) to top of metal rack. | $50-$60 |
| Crayola® Metal Display Rack | Binney & Smith | circa 1960s | Freestanding black metal rack with yellow and green "Crayola® Crayons" sign was used in store to display crayon boxes. 19in x 12in x 17in (48cm x 31cm x 43cm) and top rack is 6½in (15cm). | $20-$30 |

| ITEM | MANUFACTURER | YEAR | DESCRIPTION | ESTIMATED VALUE |
|---|---|---|---|---|
| Crayola® Metal Display Rack | Binney & Smith | circa 1960s | White metal display rack with red "Crayola® Crayons" lettering and graphics of two crayons was used to display crayon boxes. Two screw clamps on back for attaching to shelf or ledge. 26in x 5in x 2in (66cm x 13cm x 5cm). | $20-$30 |
| Crayola® Notebook | Binney & Smith | circa 1950-1960s | Small red and black leather notebook with "Crayola® Crayons" on cover was probably used by Binney & Smith salesmen. 6½in x 5¼in (17cm x 13cm). | $30-$40 |
| Binney & Smith, Inc., Common Stock Bond | Binney & Smith | 1969 | Certificate for 100 shares of Binney & Smith common stock, issued by the company in 1969. Has gold stamped seal (1953) and signature of Chairman of the Board. | $50-$80 |
| Crayola® Box Paperweight | Binney & Smith | 1977 | Pewter paperweight commemorates 75th anniversary of Crayola® crayons. 2-1/8in x 2-5/8in (5cm x 7cm). | $25-$35 |
| Binney & Smith Crayola® Watch | Binney & Smith | 1983 | Gold-plate digital watch featuring yellow and green chevron design, given to employees to commemorate the 80th birthday of Crayola® crayons. | $50-$80 |
| Crayola® Box Paperweight | Binney & Smith | 1993 | Paperweight of a Crayola® box with eight crayons sealed in an acrylic block commemorating the 90th birthday of An American Classic. 6in x 4in (15cm x 10cm). | $50-$75 |
| Crayola® 1903 Replica Stock Box | Binney & Smith | 1997 | Collector's edition is replica of 1903 stock box used in the manufacture of Crayola® crayons and contains seventy-two crayons. Picture on front of factory worker carrying original stock box with crayons. Back of box tells history of Crayola®. 9½in x 5½in x 3in (24cm x 14cm x 8cm). | $10-$15 |

### Other "Crayola®" Collectibles

| ITEM | MANUFACTURER | YEAR | DESCRIPTION | ESTIMATED VALUE |
|---|---|---|---|---|
| First Day of Issue "Celebrate The Century" Crayola® Stamp | U.S. Postal Service Binney & Smith | 1998 | 1900-1910 sheet of "Celebrate the Century" stamps includes Crayola® 32-cent stamp – February 3, 1998. | $5-$10 |
| First Day of Issue "Celebrate The Century" Cancelled Crayola® Stamp | U.S. Postal Service Binney & Smith | 1998 | Envelope has gold 32-cent stamp cancelled with "Celebrate the Century" stamp – February 3, 1998. | $15-$25 |
| First Day of Issue "Celebrate The Century" Cancelled Crayola® Stamp | U.S. Postal Service Binney & Smith | 1998 | Envelope has 32-cent stamp cancelled with "Celebrate the Century" stamp – February 3, 1998. | $5-$15 |

Note: *First Day of Issue* collectible stamps are available in a variety of styles. Values are comparable to those listed above.

| ITEM | MANUFACTURER | YEAR | DESCRIPTION | ESTIMATED VALUE |
|---|---|---|---|---|
| *North Pole Crayola® Polar Palette Art Center* | Dept. 56 Binney & Smith | 2000 | Colorful center for the arts has Crayola® crayons artfully worked into architecture. The building can be lighted with the bulb and cord that are included. 4¾in x 4¼in x 7½in (12cm x 11cm x 19cm). | $65 |
| *Crayola® Cruisin' Elves* | Dept. 56 Binney & Smith | 2000 | From the Heritage Village Collection, set of two colorful elves in crayon cars. Use to enhance the Polar Palette Art Center. | $15-$18 |
| *Leonardo and Vincent* | Dept. 56 | 2000 | From the Heritage Village Collection, two artists stand in front of an easel with artwork. Use to enhance the Polar Palette Art Center. | $15-$18 |
| Cherished Teddies Figurine – "Rosemary" with Crayola® Crayons | Priscilla Hillman/Enesco Crayola® | 2001 | "Colorful Days Are Spent With You" is limited edition figurine of little girl bear with her baby bear "doll." She is holding a picture she has drawn with Crayola® crayons, jacks and a "Fairy Tales" book on ground. 4in (10cm). | $20-$30 |
| "Happy Holidays" Plate | Binney & Smith | 2001 | Commemorative plate from Binney & Smith shows Santa in his sleigh and Crayola® products being dropped down (with parachutes) to homes in a snowy village. Diameter is 8in. (20cm). | $15-$25 |

# Category: NOVELTY ITEMS

| ITEM | MANUFACTURER | YEAR | DESCRIPTION | ESTIMATED VALUE |
|------|--------------|------|-------------|-----------------|
| Crayola® Box Table | Binney & Smith | 1981 | Child's table with folding legs, looks like a green and yellow Crayola® box. 33in x 23in (84cm x 58cm). | $50-$75 |
| Crayola® Record Player | Vanity Fair Binney & Smith | 1981 | Green and yellow record player, looks like a Crayola® crayon box. 10½in x 12¼in x 3¾in (27cm x 31cm x 10cm). | $25-$35 |
| Crayola® Men's Handkerchiefs | Binney & Smith | 1981 | "Crayola® Box" has clear top to view six "Full Sized Different Colors" of men's handkerchiefs. 6in x 6in x 1in (15cm x 15cm x 3cm). | $10-$20 |
| Crayola® Plastic Plates | Binney & Smith | 1984 | Plastic plates have colorful images of children with Crayola® crayons. Made in Italy. Diameter is approximately 8in (20cm). | $10-$20 |
| Small Crayola® Trays | Binney & Smith | 1984 | Each small plastic tray has an image of old or new Crayola® box. Approximately 6in x 4¼in (15cm x 11cm). | $5-$15 |
| Crayola® 20 Party Gift Bags | Paper Art Binney & Smith | 1984 | Twenty party gift bags look like Crayola® crayon box with Binney & Smith logo. | $5-$10 |
| Cookie Jar "Crayola Kids" | McCoy | n.d. | This authentic McCoy is often called the "Crayola" cookie jar because it has a crayon drawing of a little boy. Height is approximately 8½in (22cm). | $100+ |
| Set of four Crayola® Glasses | Binney & Smith | circa 1980s | Each glass has a front and back image of Crayola® "Different Brilliant Colors" box of eight and colorful crayons. | $20-$30 |
| Crayola® Box Pillow | Binney & Smith | circa 1980s | Novelty pillow looks like a Crayola® box of "Different Brilliant Colors." 16in x 10in (41cm x 25cm). | $15-$25 |
| Sleeping Bag | Binney & Smith | 1980s | Child's sleeping bag looks like a giant box of Crayola® crayons. | $20-$30 |
| Crayola® Ties | Binney & Smith | circa 1982-1990 | Ties with Crayola® crayons are available in several styles and colors. | $10-$15 |
| Crayola® Watches | Armitron Binney & Smith | 1984-1990s | Watches featuring Crayola® crayons are available in assorted styles and colors. | $10-$30 |
| Crayola® Wall Clock | Armitron Binney & Smith | circa 1984-1990s | Crayola® wall clock is available in several primary colors. Quartz clock has second hand. Diameter is 10in (25cm). | $15-$25 |
| Crayola® Aquarium | Binney & Smith | 1990 | Aquarium is shaped like a Crayola® crayon. Height is 21in (53cm). | $15-$25 |
| Crayola® Lamps | Binney & Smith | circa 1990 | Crayola® lamps are available in a variety of sizes and styles. | $10-$20 |
| So Big® Crayon | Binney & Smith | circa 1990 | Giant plastic crayon (available in red, blue, yellow and green) with a real paper label measures fifteen times the actual size of a Crayola® crayon. 4½ft (1.4m). | $30 |
| Crayola® Lip Glosses | Avon Binney & Smith | circa 1990s | "Crayola® box" contains three lip gloss crayon sticks. Box is approximately 3in x 2in x ½in (8cm x 5cm x 1cm). | $5-$15 |
| Inflatable Crayola® Crayon | Binney & Smith | circa 1990s | Large Crayola® blow-up balloon is available in several colors. Height is approximately 46in (116cm). | $5-$10 |
| Crayola® Drum and Mallet Set | Remco Binney & Smith | circa 1990s | Percussion "doodle drum" says: "National Grammy Concert Series for Children." Has treble and bass music staffs on drum and includes mallet with rubber tip. Diameter of drum is 10in (25cm). | $30-$50 |
| Crayola® License Plate | Binney & Smith | 1990s | Crayola® license plates can be found in a variety of styles and colors. | $10-$20 |
| Crayola® Wind-Up Clock® | Spartus Binney & Smith | 1991 | Bright yellow wind-up clock has red bells on top with crayon drawing on face. Height is approximately 7in (18cm). | $10-$15 |

| ITEM | MANUFACTURER | YEAR | DESCRIPTION | ESTIMATED VALUE |
|---|---|---|---|---|
| Crayola® Plastic Display Tray | Binney & Smith | 1992 | Yellow plastic tray with bright pink Crayola® crayon on front has screw clamps for attaching to shelf or window ledge. Approximately 23½in x 4½in. x 3in (50cm x 12cm x 8cm). | $15-$20 |
| Crayola® Night Light | Binney & Smith | 1993 | Crayon night light is available in several colors. Has an on/off switch and plugs into wall. 5in (13cm). | $5-$10 |
| Crayola® Box Night Light | Binney & Smith | 1993 | Night light looks like a box of Crayola® crayons. Has an on/off switch and plugs into wall. 4in x 3in x 1½in (10cm x 8cm x 4cm). | $5-$10 |
| Bathroom Set | Village Binney & Smith | circa 1993 | Toothpaste holder and soap dish have Crayola® crayon and box images. | $10-$15 |
| "Crayola® Rocks" AM/FM Radio | ISIS Electronics Binney & Smith | 1994 | AM/FM radio looks like a box of Crayola® crayons. Distributed in Australia. Approximately 3¾in x 2¾in x 1in (10cm x 7cm x 3cm). | $10-$20 |
| Crayola® Box Calculator | Advanced Concepts Binney & Smith | 1994 | Green and yellow "Crayola® box" opens to show a calculator. 3¾in x 3½in x 1½in (10cm x 9cm x 4cm). | $10-$15 |
| Crayola® Child's Umbrella | Binney & Smith | 1997 | Multicolored child's umbrella with cover. Covers are available in several colors. 21in (53cm). | $5-$8 |
| Crayola® Mailbox Bank | Gearbox Binney & Smith | circa 1998 | Replica of a United States mailbox, green and yellow with Crayola® logo. Bank includes lock and key. Approximately 7in (18cm). | $15-$20 |
| Crayola® Room Thermometer | Morco Binney & Smith | circa 1999 | White room thermometer has Crayola® crayon and Binney & Smith logos. Approximately 11in (28cm). | $10-$15 |
| Crayola® Easel | Hallmark Binney & Smith | 1999 | Bright pastel Crayola® crayon easel includes clear plastic picture frame. 5in x 7in (13cm x 18cm). | $10-$15 |
| Crayola® Table and Chair Set | Hallmark | 1999 | Small Crayola® table (12in [31cm]) and chair (9½in [24cm]) set are the perfect size for the Crayola® bears. | $20-$30 |
| Crayola® Desk Set | Binney & Smith | 1999 | Stapler, pencil holder and tape dispenser, bright red with "Tip." Each item sold separately. | $8-$10 |
| Cube Crayola® Snooze Clock with AM/FM Radio | Polyconcept, USA Binney & Smith | 1999 | AM/FM radio and snooze cube clock is bright red and yellow with antennae. | $10-$15 |
| Crayola® Night Light Lamp | Binney & Smith | circa 2000 | Crayola® night light and lamp combination has a yellow crayon base and colorful lampshade. Built-in rainbow disc projects color on the ceiling of the room. Approximately 15in (38cm). | $50 |

# Category: ORNAMENTS and MINIATURES

**Holiday Collection Ornaments**

| ITEM | MANUFACTURER | YEAR | DESCRIPTION | ESTIMATED VALUE |
|---|---|---|---|---|
| *Bright Christmas Dreams* | Hallmark Holiday Collection | 1987 | Four mice sleep in Crayola® box. | $80-$90 |
| *Teacher* | Hallmark Holiday Collection | 1988 | White rabbit draws picture of a carrot in red book with a Crayola® crayon. | $20 |
| *Bright Journey* | Hallmark Keepsake Holiday Series #1 | 1989 | Bear sitting on raft made of Crayola® crayons. | $65 |
| *Bright Moving Colors* | Hallmark Keepsake Holiday Series #2 | 1990 | White mouse drives a Crayola® box sleigh. | $50 |
| Felt Crayola® Bear Ornament | Hallmark | 1990 | Red felt bear wears red Crayola® shirt and has ribbon hanger. 4½in (12cm). | $10-$15 |
| *Bright Vibrant Carols* | Hallmark Keepsake Holiday Series #3 | 1991 | Red bear playing Crayola® box organ with crayon pipes. | $40-$45 |
| *Bright Blazing Colors* | Hallmark Keepsake Holiday Series #4 | 1992 | Dalmatian drives Crayola® box fire truck. | $40 |

| ITEM | MANUFACTURER | YEAR | DESCRIPTION | ESTIMATED VALUE |
|---|---|---|---|---|
| Bear with Crayola® Drum | Binney & Smith | 1992 | Plastic brown bear plays drum with red and green Crayola® crayons. Ornament was included in 1992 Christmas tin. 3¼in (8cm). | $5 |
| *Bright Shining Castle* | Hallmark Keepsake Holiday Series #5 | 1993 | Bear plays trumpet in front of Crayola® box castle. | $30-$35 |
| *Bright Playful Colors* | Hallmark Keepsake Holiday Series #6 | 1994 | Bear sits in swing made of Crayola® crayons. | $30-$35 |
| *Bright 'n' Sunny Tepee* | Hallmark Keepsake Holiday Series #7 | 1995 | Bear peeks from tepee made of crayons. | $25 |
| *Colorful World* | Hallmark Holiday Collection | 1995 | Mouse with Crayola® crayon sits on top of multicultural crayon box. | $25-$30 |
| *Bright Flying Colors* | Hallmark Keepsake Holiday Series #8 | 1996 | White mouse flies in airplane made of Crayola® crayons. | $25-$30 |
| *Bright Rocking Colors* | Hallmark Keepsake Holiday Series #9 | 1997 | Bear with cowboy hat sits on a "Crayola® box" rocking horse. | $30 |
| *Bright Sledding Colors* (Final in Series) | Hallmark Keepsake Holiday Series #10 | 1998 | Bear holding Crayola® crayon rides on sled. | $20-$25 |
| *Clownin' Around* | Hallmark Holiday Collection | 1999 | Juggling clown rides a unicycle. | $20-$25 |
| *Backpack Bear* | Hallmark Holiday Collection | 2000 | Blown glass bear with beanie wears a backpack. Gold with glitter. | $40-$45 |
| *King of the Ring* | Hallmark Holiday Collection | 2000 | Circus lion sits on Crayola® pedestal. | $20-$25 |
| *Color Crew Chief* | Hallmark Holiday Collection | 2001 | Santa's elf holds a gold ornament and Crayola® crayon. | $10-$15 |
| *Rainbow Snowman* | Hallmark Holiday Collection | 2002 | Snowman has Crayola® scarf and crayons for arms. | $10-$15 |
| **Spring Collection Ornaments and Figurines** | | | | |
| *Crayola® Bunny* | Hallmark Spring Collection | 1992 | Painter Bunny wears overalls and holds a Crayola® crayon and egg. | $35 |
| *Colorful Spring* | Hallmark Spring Collection | 1993 | White rabbit with carrot sits in swing made of Crayola® crayons. | $30-$35 |
| *Picture Perfect* | Hallmark Spring Collection | 1995 | White artist rabbit is drawing on easel with Crayola® crayon. | $20 |
| *Hippity-Hop Delivery* | Hallmark Spring Collection | 1996 | White rabbit pushes Crayola® wheelbarrow filled with eggs. | $15-$20 |
| *Eggs-pert Artist* | Hallmark Spring Collection | 1997 | Rabbit sits on spoon and is decorating blue Crayola® egg. | $20 |
| Pastel Bunny with Egg | Hallmark | 1989 | Flocked pastel bunny holds a "Crayola®" egg. PVC bunnies are available in lavender, peach, light blue, yellow and pink. 2¾in (7cm). | $5-$10 |
| Crayola® Bunny Egg Holder Figurine | Hallmark | 1990 | Painter Bunny wears overalls and yellow painter's cap and pulls a cart with decorated egg. | $5-$10 |
| Crayola® Bunny Figurine | Hallmark | 1991 | Plastic Crayola® Bunny and Candy Cotton Tail hold a basket between them. | $5-$10 |
| Crayola® Bunny Easter Eggspress Figurine | Hallmark | 1993 | Plastic Crayola® Bunny and Candy Cotton Tail drive train. | $5-$10 |
| Crayola® Bear Figurines | Binney & Smith | circa 1990s | PVC Crayola® bear holds a Crayola® crayon. Bears are available in red, yellow, blue, green, orange and purple. Approximately 3¼in (8cm). | $5-$10 |
| **Hallmark Miniatures** | | | | |
| Crayola® Snow Globe | Hallmark Binney & Smith | 1999 | Small snow globe has castle inside and says "Color Your Day Happy." | $10-$15 |
| *Booker Beanie* (9th in "Happy Hatters" Series) | Hallmark Merry Miniatures | 2000 | Little boy in beanie cap holds lunchbox and apple. | $5-$10 |

| ITEM | MANUFACTURER | YEAR | DESCRIPTION | ESTIMATED VALUE |
|---|---|---|---|---|
| *Bee Bright* (9th in "Bee" Series) | Hallmark Merry Miniatures | 2001 | Bumblebee draws on notebook paper with red Crayola® crayon. | $5-$10 |
| *Booker Bear* (9th in "Itty Bitty Bears" Series) | Hallmark Merry Miniatures | 2002 | Little bear with moveable arms and cap has "ABC" and "123" on feet. Holds box of Crayola® crayons. | $5-$10 |
| **Other Miniatures** | | | | |
| Miniature Crayola® Box 8 | Binney & Smith | circa 1998 | Tiny green and yellow box, open to show eight Crayola® crayons, is dollhouse accessory. Approximately ½in x ¼in (1cm x .65cm). | $5-$10 |
| Miniature Crayola® Box 64 | Binney & Smith | circa 2000 | Tiny green and yellow box of sixty-four Crayola® crayons is dollhouse accessory. Approximately 3/8in x ½in (.9cm x 1cm). | $5-$10 |
| Miniature Crayola® Box with Eight Crayons by Darrel Irwin | Binney & Smith | 2002 | Green and yellow box with eight actual Crayola® crayons that can be removed from box. Approximately 1in x 1½in (3cm x 4cm). | $40-$65 |

# Category: PAINTS and PAINT TINS

**Paint Tins and Trays**

| ITEM | MANUFACTURER | YEAR | DESCRIPTION | ESTIMATED VALUE |
|---|---|---|---|---|
| Artista® Frescol Compact Colors Tin | Binney & Smith | circa 1936 | Black and gold single tin includes five colors. 8½in x 2in x ½in (22cm x 5cm x 1cm). | $20-$30 |
| Artista® Water Color Tin | Binney & Smith | 1940s | No. 03. Round water color tin is yellow and black with three sections. Middle section is for mixing colors. Diameter is 5½in (14cm). | $100-$175 |
| Playtime Water Colors Tray | Binney & Smith | circa 1940s | Blue and white cardboard box (single tray) has picture of lamb and giraffe. Approximately 8½in x 2in x ½in (22cm x 5cm x 1cm). | $20-$30 |
| Playtime Water Colors Tin | Binney & Smith | circa 1940s | Red and white single tin has picture of toy soldier, drum and other toys. Approximately 8in x 2in x ½in (20cm x 5cm x 1cm). | $20-$30 |
| Water Colors Tin | Binney & Smith | 1941 | Dark green and silver single tin has sailboat and seagulls. (Binney & Smith name is on inside of tray only.) 8in x 2in x ½in (20cm x 5cm x 1cm). | $20-$30 |
| Arcadian Water Colors Tin | Binney & Smith | 1940-1950s | No. 525. Red and white single tin has picture of sailboat and lighthouse. 8in x 2in x ½in (20cm x 5cm x 1cm). | $15-$25 |
| Artista® Water Colors | Binney & Smith | circa 1948 | Black single tin with gold letters says: "Makers of Crayola®." 8½in x 2in x ½in (22cm x 5cm x 1cm). | $15-$20 |
| Artista® Water Colors | Binney & Smith | circa 1948 | Black double tin with gold letters saying "Makers of Crayola®." Approximately 8½in x 3in x ½in (22cm x 8cm x 1cm). | $15-$25 |
| Artista® Water Colors | Binney & Smith | circa 1953 | No. 09. Blue and beige single tin has graphic design and Gold Medal logo. 8½in x 2in x ½in (22cm x 5cm x 1cm). | $10-$15 |
| Artista® Water Colors | Binney & Smith | circa 1953 | No. 16. Blue and beige double tin has graphic design and Gold Medal logo. Approximately 8in x 3in x ½in (20 cm x 8cm x 1cm). | $10-$20 |
| Playtime Water Colors Tin | Binney & Smith | 1953 | No. 515. Red single tin has white lettering and graphics of animals. 8in x 2in x ½in (20cm x 5cm x 1cm). | $10-$15 |
| Playtime Water Colors Tin | Binney & Smith | 1957 | No. 515. Orange single tin has white lettering and graphics of picture of monkeys. Price: 25 cents. 8in x 2in x ½in (20cm x 5cm x 1cm). | $10-$15 |
| Arcadian Water Colors Tin | Binney & Smith | 1957 | No. 525. Red and white single tin has stick people at easel. 8in x 2in x ½in (20cm x 5cm x 1cm). | $10-$15 |
| Playtime Water Colors | Binney & Smith | circa 1959 | No. 515. Plastic purple, blue and white single tray. Non-toxic. 8¾in x 2¼in x ¾in (22cm x 6cm x 2cm). | $5-$10 |

| ITEM | MANUFACTURER | YEAR | DESCRIPTION | ESTIMATED VALUE |
|---|---|---|---|---|
| Crayola® Water Colors | Binney & Smith | circa 1959 | No. 080. Plastic Crayola® single tray is green, yellow and white. CP (Certified Products), non-toxic. 8¾in x 2¼in x ¾in (22cm x 6cm x 2cm). | $5-$10 |
| Peacock® Water Colors | Binney & Smith | 1959-1960s | The "Peacock®" brand was originally made by the Canadian Crayon Company and later purchased by Binney & Smith. Plastic tray is dark red and white. 8¾in x 2¼in x ¾in (22cm x 6cm x 2cm). | $5-$10 |
| Playtime Water Colors Tin | Binney & Smith | 1960 | No. 515. Blue and yellow single tin has picture of children. Price: 29 cents. 8½in x 2in x ½in (22cm x 5cm x 1cm). | $5-$10 |
| Playtime Water Colors Tin | Binney & Smith | 1960 | No. 550. Blue and yellow double tin has picture of children. Price: 69 cents. Approximately 8½in x 3¼in x ½in (22cm x 8cm x 1cm). | $10-$15 |
| Arcadian Water Colors Tin | Binney & Smith | 1960s | No. 625. Double tin has geometric shapes on a seesaw. (Also available in plastic paint tray.) Approximately 8½in x 3¼in x ½in (22cm x 8cm x 1cm). | $10-$20 |
| Artista® Water Colors | Binney & Smith | 1960s | No. 08. Aqua and white single tin says: "New! Improved!" 8½in x 2in x ½in (22cm x 5cm x 1cm). | $5-$10 |
| Artista® Opaque Water Colors | Binney & Smith | 1960s | No. 508. Dark green and white double tin with red "NEW" and "OPAQUE." Approximately 8in x 3in x ½in (20cm x 8cm x 1cm). | $10-$20 |

### Other Paints

| ITEM | MANUFACTURER | YEAR | DESCRIPTION | ESTIMATED VALUE |
|---|---|---|---|---|
| Artista® Flexola Paint | Binney & Smith | circa 1948 | Gold Medal Products – "Sample to Test" includes four tubes of paint in small gold box. "Makers of Crayola®." Box measures 3¼in x 3½in x 1in (8cm x 9cm x 3cm). | $10-$20 |
| Artista® Powder Paint Canister | Binney & Smith | 1953 | Green and yellow powder paint can "for easel work & decorative design for school and home." 1 lb (.45 kg). | $5-$10 |
| Genie Handipaint Canister | Binney & Smith | 1953 | Black and white powder paint can has metal "sprinkle powder" top. 8 oz (236.6 ml). | $5-$10 |
| Crayola® Finger Paint Powder | Binney & Smith | 1958-1970s | No. 1800. Crayola® powder finger paint in round cardboard container with metal top which has holes for pouring. 8 oz (236.6 ml). | $5-$10 |
| Driad Powder Paint | Binney & Smith | 1958-1970s | Red and white powder paint can "for easel and mural painting & craft work." 1 lb (.45 kg) | $5-$10 |
| Tem-pra-tone® | Binney & Smith | 1970s | No. 830. White plastic squeeze bottle with red top and blue lettering. 8 oz (236.6 ml). | $5-$8 |

Note: Tempera, finger paint and other powder paints were sold in a variety of colors. Values are comparable to those listed above.

# Category: PINS and MAGNETS

### Pins

| ITEM | MANUFACTURER | YEAR | DESCRIPTION | ESTIMATED VALUE |
|---|---|---|---|---|
| "Collect Crayola® Crayons & Markers" Pin | Binney & Smith | circa 1980s | Pin features the dark green and yellow box with six Crayola® crayons. 3in x 2in (8cm x 5cm). | $5-$15 |
| Crayola® Crayon Box Lapel Pin | Binney & Smith | 1990s | Promotional item from Binney & Smith, a metal pin with green and yellow Crayola® box and five crayons (no labels on crayons) and has small gold insignia below "Crayola® Crayons." 1in x ½in (3cm x 1cm). | $15-$20 |
| Crayola® Crayon Box Lapel Pin | Binney & Smith | 1990s | Promotional item from Binney & Smith, a metal pin with green and yellow Crayola® box and five crayons (labels have serpentine design). Lower right corner has ® trademark. 1in x ½in (3cm x 1cm). | $15-$20 |
| Crayola® Crayon Box Pin | Binney & Smith | circa 1995 | Promotional item from Binney & Smith, a cardboard Crayola® box with five colorful crayons. 2in x 1in (5cm x 3cm). | $10-$15 |

| ITEM | MANUFACTURER | YEAR | DESCRIPTION | ESTIMATED VALUE |
|---|---|---|---|---|
| Crayola® Stamp Lapel Pin | U.S. Postal Service Binney & Smith | circa 1998 | Metal pin features the "Celebrate the Century" 1903 box of Crayola® crayons on 32-cent postage stamp. Pin has clear plastic seal. 1in x 1in (3cm x 3cm). | $5-$8 |
| Crayola® Stamp Lapel Pin | Winco International U.S. Postal Service Binney & Smith | circa 1998 | Metal pin features the "Celebrate the Century" 1903 box of Crayola® crayons on 32-cent postage stamp. 1in x 1in (3cm x 3cm). | $5-$8 |
| Crayola® Crayons 8 Box Pin | Binney & Smith | circa 1999 | Promotional item from Binney & Smith, a cardboard Crayola® box with eight colorful crayons. "Certified Non-Toxic" and has the open "smile" design. 2in x 1in (5cm x 3cm). | $10-$15 |
| Crayola® "Tip" Pennant Pin | Binney & Smith | circa 1999 | White plastic pin pennant has yellow "Tip" waving. Approximately 1¼in x 3¼in (3cm x 8cm). | $3-$5 |
| Special Edition – NAEA Crayola® Dream-Makers® Pin | Binney & Smith | 1999 | Pin features little girl with sunflowers and was given to members of the National Art Education Association at the 1999 convention. Pin reads "Crayola® Dream-Makers®" and Congratulations NAEA on 50 years!" 3in x 2in (8cm x 5cm). | $5-$10 |
| Crayola® Dream-Makers® Lapel Pin | Binney & Smith | 1999 | Metal pin has image of a family on a hillside looking at the blue sky. "Crayola® Dream-Makers® 1999." 1¼in x 1¼in (3cm x 3cm). | $5-$10 |
| "Crayola® – It Starts Here" Pins | Binney & Smith | circa 2000 | Promotional items from Binney & Smith feature four different ads that emphasize the importance of arts education to a child's overall development and learning. 3in x 2in (8cm x 5cm). | $5-$8 |
| Crayola® Store Holiday Pins | Binney & Smith | 2001 | Round (3in [8cm] diameter) and rectangular pins read "The Crayola® Store – Have a Colorful Holiday." 1¾in x 2¾in (5cm x 7cm). | $3-$5 |
| Crayola® Star Pin | Binney & Smith | 2001 | Promotional item from Binney & Smith has a small round mirror on yellow star and says "Creativity" and "Crayola® – It Starts Here." Approximately 2¼in x 2¼in (6cm x 6cm). | $5-$10 |
| **Magnets** | | | | |
| Crayola® Crayon Box Magnet | Binney & Smith | 1990s | Crayola® box rubberized magnet has five bright crayons in open box. 2½in x 1½in (6cm x 4cm). | $5-$8 |
| Crayola® Crayon Box Magnet | Binney & Smith | 1990s | Plastic Crayola® box magnet has eight "Different Brilliant Colors" in open box. 2½in x 1¼in (6cm x 3cm). | $5-$10 |
| Crayola® Stamp Magnet | U.S. Postal Service Binney & Smith | 1998 | Magnet has black background with colorful squiggles that can be punched out and used as a frame. Center features the "Celebrate the Century" 1903 box of Crayola® crayons on 32-cent postage stamp. Approximately 6in x 5in (15cm x 13cm). | $5-$8 |
| Crayola® Stamp Magnet | U.S. Postal Service Binney & Smith | 1998 | Magnet has black background with colorful squiggles and features the "Celebrate the Century" 1903 box of Crayola® crayons on 32-cent postage stamp. 2½in x 2½in (6cm x 6cm). | $5 |
| Crayola® Box Foam Magnet | Hallmark Binney & Smith | 1999 | 3-D foam magnet features "smile" 24 box that contains five colorful Crayola® crayons. 4in x 2¼in (10cm x 6cm). | $5-$8 |
| "Tip" in Airplane Foam Magnet | Hallmark Binney & Smith | 1999 | 3-D foam magnet features red "Tip" in airplane. Approximately 3½in x 4in (9cm x 10cm). | $5-$8 |
| Acrylic Crayola® Crayon Magnet | Hallmark Binney & Smith | 1999 | Magnet is a red Crayola® crayon sealed in an acrylic block. (Also available in other primary colors.) 2¾in x ¾in x ¾in (7cm x 2cm x 2cm). | $5-$10 |
| Crayola® Crayon Frame Magnet | Hallmark Binney & Smith | 1999 | Magnet frame is made of four pastel Crayola® crayons. 2¼in x 2in (6cm x 5cm). | $5 |
| Crayola® Pastel Crayon Magnets | Hallmark Binney & Smith | 1999 | Plastic Crayola® crayons are available in a variety of pastel colors. 2½in x ¾in (6cm x 2cm). | $3-$5 |
| Red "Tip" Magnet | Binney & Smith | 1999 | Plastic red "Tip" is waving and wears blue and white tennis shoes. 3in (8cm). | $5-$8 |

# Category: PUZZLES

| ITEM | MANUFACTURER | YEAR | DESCRIPTION | ESTIMATED VALUE |
|---|---|---|---|---|
| *Shades of Childhood!* | Springbok Hallmark | circa 1980s | Puzzle of rows of Crayola® crayons without labels, has 500 pieces. 18in x 23½in (46cm x 60cm). | $10-$20 |
| *Color Your World* | Eaton | 1983 | Puzzle of alternating rows of Crayola® crayons with labels, has more than 500 pieces. 18in x 24in (46cm x 61cm). | $10-$20 |
| *Crayola® Freeway!* | Springbok Binney & Smith | 1986 | Puzzle of Crayola® crayons lined up to look like a freeway, has 1000 pieces. 24in x 30in (61cm x 76cm). | $10-$20 |
| *Bear Brigade* | Springbok Hallmark | circa 1986 | Children's puzzle of Crayola® bears, has forty-eight pieces. 12in x 17in (31cm x 43cm). | $10-$15 |
| Crayola® Jigsaw Puzzle (*Octopus under the Ocean*) | Milton Bradley Binney & Smith | circa 1990s | Children's puzzle of octopus with Crayola® crayons, has twenty-four pieces. 12½in x 15in (32cm x 38cm). | $5-$10 |
| Crayola® Jigsaw Puzzle (*Crayola® Castle*) | Binney & Smith | circa 1990s | Children's puzzle of castle made of Crayola® crayons, has twenty-four pieces. 12½in x 15in (32cm x 38cm). | $5-$10 |
| FREE Crayola® Factory Puzzle | Binney & Smith | 1992 | Puzzle of Crayola® factory team making crayons, has 100 pieces. 9in x 12in (23cm x 31cm). | $5-$10 |
| *Crayola® School Days* | Springbok Binney & Smith | 1994 | Puzzle of collage of old Crayola® school supplies, has 500 pieces. 18 in x 23.5 in (45.7 cm x 59.7 cm) | $10-$20 |
| *Crayola® Clownin' Around* Jigsaw Puzzle | Hallmark Binney & Smith | 1999 | Double-sided puzzle with clown ornament on one side and Crayola® crayon pattern on other, has eighty pieces. 8in x 10in (20cm x 25cm). | $5-$10 |
| Crayola® Crayon Jigsaw Puzzle | Hallmark Binney & Smith | 1999 | Puzzle of randomly arranged Crayola® crayons, has 100 pieces. Approximately 13½in x 19in (34cm x 48cm). | $10 |

# Category: TINS - OLD and NEW

| ITEM | MANUFACTURER | YEAR | DESCRIPTION | ESTIMATED VALUE |
|---|---|---|---|---|
| An-Du-Septic® Dustless Blackboard Crayon Tin | Binney & Smith | 1928-1940s | Black tin with green and gold graphics: "Dustless Blackboard Crayon." One gross. 6in x 3½in x 3½in (15cm x 9cm x 9cm). | $15-$30 |
| An-Du-Septic® Dustless Crayon Tin | Binney & Smith | 1928-1940s | Black tin with green and gold graphics: "Dustless Crayon." One gross. 6in x 3½in x 3½in (15cm x 9cm x 9cm). | $15-$30 |
| Anti-Dust® Pure Chalk Crayon Tin | Binney & Smith | 1930-1940s | Brown tin with beige and red graphics: "Anti-Dust® Pure Chalk Crayon." One gross. 6in x 3½in x 3½in (15cm x 9cm x 9cm). | $15-$30 |
| Anti-Dust® Pure Chalk Crayon Tin | Binney & Smith | 1930-1940s | Rare black tin with green graphics: "Anti-Dust® Pure Chalk Crayon." One gross. 6in x 3½in x 3½in (15cm x 9cm x 9cm). | $50-$75 |
| An-Du-Septic® Dustless Crayon Tin | Binney & Smith | Early 1940s | Gray striped tin with orange top – "The Approved Dustless Crayon for Class & Lecture Room Use." One gross. Gold Medal logo. 6in x 3½in x 3½in (15cm x 9cm x 9cm). | $15-$30 |
| Colored Crayons Tin | Binney & Smith | circa 1927 | Small black and gold tin with hinged top includes eight "Crayola®" crayons. "GOLD MEDAL CRAYONS FOR EVERY USE (Trademark)." 3¾in x 2¾in x 3/8in (10cm x 7cm x .9cm). | $20-$30 |
| Colored Drawing Crayons Tin | Binney & Smith | 1941 | Small black and gold tin with hinged top includes eight sticks. "GOLD MEDAL PRODUCTS." 3in x 3¾in x 3/8in (8cm x 10cm x .9cm). | $20-$30 |
| 8 Brilliant Colored Crayons Tin | Binney & Smith | 1948-1960s | Small green and yellow tin with hinged top includes eight Crayola® crayons. 3in x 4in x 3/8in (8cm x 10cm x .9cm). "Chevron" logo was first used on this style tin on January 31, 1947. | $10-$20 |
| 8 Brilliant Colored Crayons Tin | Binney & Smith | 1948-1960s | Small green and yellow tin with hinged top includes eight Perma crayons. 3in x 4in x 3/8in (8cm x 10cm x .9cm). | $10-$20 |

| ITEM | MANUFACTURER | YEAR | DESCRIPTION | ESTIMATED VALUE |
|------|--------------|------|-------------|-----------------|
| Colored Drawing Crayons Tin | Binney & Smith | 1953 | Small red and white tin with hinged top includes eight sticks of crayons. 3in x 3¾in x 3/8in (8cm x 10cm x .9cm). | $15-$25 |
| (Note: With the onset of World War II and the shortage of metal, these tins began disappearing in the mid-1940s. Binney & Smith began making new collectible tins in the 1980s.) | | | | |
| Gold Medal School Crayons Tin | Binney & Smith | 1982 | Round red tin is replica of 1903 Crayola® box design with matte finish. Approximate height is 6in (15cm). | $15-$20 |
| Crayola® Hot Air Balloon Tin | Binney & Smith | 1983 | Round tin has blue lid with squirrel and picture of animals in a hot air balloon and crayon box. Approximate height is 6in (15cm). | $150-$200 |
| Crayola® Watch Tin | Armitron Binney & Smith | circa 1984 | Green and yellow tin with lift-off lid has picture of Crayola® box on lid. "The Original Crayola® Armitron Collectibles." Approximately 2½in x 5½in x ¾in (6cm x 14cm x 2cm). | $3-$5 |
| Crayola® Circus Pedestal Tin | Heartland Binney & Smith | 1989 | White and purple tin is shaped like a round circus pedestal with colorful graphics of animals circling the ring. Height is 4in (10cm). Top diameter is 5in (13cm) and bottom diameter is 7¾in (20cm). | $100-$150 |
| Crayola® Marker Parker | Binney & Smith | 1990 | Round black and white checked tin with neon graphics, made for storing Crayola® markers. Approximate height is 6in (15cm). | $10-$15 |
| Crayola® 52 Ultimate Pencil Collection Tin | Binney & Smith Europe | 1990s | No. 3652. Huge flat tin has pictures of the world with hot air balloon, panda, penguins, kangaroo and others on blue background. Includes fifty-two "coloured" pencils, two sketching pencils, eraser and sharpener. "Featuring a double easel for simple 'colour' selection." 17¼in x 10¼in x 5/8in (44cm x 27cm x 2cm). | $45-$75 |
| Crayola® 8 Tin | Binney & Smith Germany | 1990s | Yellow and green tin with hinged top has large purple crayon on front. Includes eight large crayons and has German description on back. 5½in x 4in x ¾in (14cm x 10cm x 2cm). | $20-$30 |
| Crayola® Art Tools Playing Cards Tin | Bicycle Binney & Smith | 1990s | Small red tin with silver lift-off lid includes playing cards with art tools and special craft ideas. 3¼in x 4¼in x 1in (8cm x 11cm x 3cm). | $5-$10 |
| Crayola® Collector's Colors Limited Edition | Binney & Smith | 1991 | Green tin and yellow with old trademark graphics on lid and historical descriptions on four sides. Includes replica of original eight retired colors. 5in x 7in x 2¼in (13cm x 18cm x 6cm). | $10-$15 |
| Crayola® Crayon Tin | Binney & Smith | 1991 | White and aqua hinged-top tin features colorful crayons. 4¼in x 7¾in x 1¼in (11cm x 20cm x 3cm). | $10-$20 |
| Crayola® Christmas Tin | Binney & Smith | 1992 | Red United States version (square) children under tree – comes with bear ornament. 6in x 6in x 2¾in (15cm x 15cm x 7cm). | $5-$10 |
| Crayola® Christmas Tin | Binney & Smith Canada | 1993 | Red tin is Canadian version (rectangular) children under tree. Approximately 4½in x 7¾in x 2¼in (12cm x 20cm x 1cm). | $30-$50 |
| Crayola® 90th Anniversary Tin | Binney & Smith | 1993 | Green tin has eight crayons on the lid with "1903-1993" and historical descriptions on four sides. 6in x 6in x 2¾in (15cm x 15cm x 7cm). | $10-$15 |
| Childhood Memories Tin | Binney & Smith | 1994 | Green and rose tin has a picture of Grandmother with two children – "Childhood memories that last a lifetime." 6in x 6in x 2¾in (15cm x 15cm x 7cm). | $10-$15 |
| Crayola® 64 Tin | Binney & Smith | 1995 | Green and yellow box of sixty-four Crayola® crayons with "Tips" climbing and tumbling out of top. 6in x 6in x 2¾in (15cm x 15cm x 7cm). | $10-$15 |
| World of Coloring Fun Tin | Binney & Smith | 1995 | Green and yellow "World of Coloring Fun!" World with yellow "Tip." 6in x 6in x 2¾in (15cm x 15cm x 7cm). | $10-$15 |
| National Basketball Association (NBA) | Binney & Smith Canada | 1995 | Black tin with basketball action shot and team logos around sides. 4½in x 7¾in x 2¼in (12cm x 20cm x 6cm). | $10-$20 |

| ITEM | MANUFACTURER | YEAR | DESCRIPTION | ESTIMATED VALUE |
|---|---|---|---|---|
| National Hockey Association (NHA) | Binney & Smith Canada | 1995 | Action shot on lid with team logos around sides. Includes twelve color markers with team names and logos. 4½in x 7¾in x 2¼in (12cm x 20cm x 6cm). | $10-$20 |
| Peace Tin | Hallmark Binney & Smith | 1995 | Light blue "PEACE" tin with pastel animals around world. 8in x 6in x 4½in (20cm x 15cm x 12cm). | $30-$60 |
| Gold Medal School Crayons Tin | Binney & Smith | 1995 | Round red tin has replica of 1903 Crayola® box design with shiny finish. Tin was used as a school fundraiser and has an approximate height of 6in (15cm). | $15-$20 |
| 101 Dalmatians | Binney & Smith Canada | 1996 | Disney's 101 Dalmatians tin is white with black "spots." 4½in x 7¾in x 2¼in (12cm x 20cm x 6cm). | $15-$25 |
| True Blue Heroes Limited Edition | Binney & Smith | 1997 | Flat tin with hinged top includes nine special Crayola® crayons. 5½in x 5in x ½in (14cm x 13cm x 1cm). | $15-$20 |
| Caldor Tin | Binney & Smith | 1997 | Red and green tin shows three dreaming children. Includes forty-eight Crayola® crayons. Distributed in Australia. 4½in x 7¾in x 2¼in (12cm x 20cm x 6cm). | $15-$25 |
| Crayola® "Colour" Keeper | Binney & Smith | 1997 | Small tin with hinged top includes sixteen Crayola® crayons. Distributed in United Kingdom. 1¼in x 3¼in x 4in (3cm x 8cm x 10cm). | $20-$30 |
| Crayons Á La Cire | Binney & Smith | 1997 | Small tin with hinged top includes sixteen Crayola® crayons. Distributed in Europe/France. 1¼in x 3½in x 4in (3cm x 9cm x 10cm). | $20-$30 |
| Colorful Jungle Discovery Series No. 1 | Binney & Smith | 1997 | Crayola® crayons in jungle scene. Distributed in Australia. 4½in x 7¾in x 2¼in (12cm x 20cm x 6cm). | $10-$15 |
| Ocean Dive Limited Edition No. 2 | Binney & Smith | 1997 | Small tin with hinged top features orange "Tip" in ocean with fish. Distributed in Australia. 1½in x 3¾in x 4in (4cm x 8cm x 10cm). | $5-$10 |
| Space Walk Limited Edition No. 3 | Binney & Smith | 1997 | Small tin with hinged top features yellow "Tip" in outer space. Distributed in Australia. 1½in x 3¾in x 4in (4cm x 8cm x 10cm). | $5-$10 |
| Jungle Safari Limited Edition No. 4 | Binney & Smith | 1998 | Small tin with hinged top features red "Tip" in jungle with snake and giraffe. Distributed in Australia. 1½in x 3¾in x 4in (4cm x 8cm x 10cm). | $5-$10 |
| Desert Oasis Limited Edition No. 5 | Binney & Smith | 1998 | Small tin with hinged top features green "Tip" in desert with camel. Distributed in Australia. 1½in x 3¾in x 4in (4cm x 8cm x 10cm). | $5-$10 |
| Arctic Tin | Hallmark Binney & Smith | 1998 | Blue and white tin features polar bears with igloo. 4½in x 7¾in x 2¼in (12cm x 20cm x 6cm). | $10-$15 |
| Gold Medal School Crayons Tin | Binney & Smith | 1998 | Round red tin is replica of 1903 Crayola® box design. Tin has matte finish. Approximate height is 6in (15cm). | $10-$20 |
| 40th Anniversary Crayola® Crayons | Hallmark Binney & Smith | 1998 | Bright yellow tin reads "Limited Edition – History of 64 box with sharpener – 1958; and retired crayons in 1990." 6in x 6in x 2¾in (15cm x 15cm x 7cm). | $10-$20 |
| Crayola® Big Box of Ideas | Binney & Smith | 1998 | Green and yellow tin with "Tip" and assorted tools, includes craft ideas for using Crayola® crayons, pencils and other items. 6in x 3½in x 4in (15cm x 9cm x 10cm). | $15-$20 |
| Christmas Carols | Hallmark Binney & Smith | 1999 | Round dark green tin with red top features Christmas carolers that are crayons and markers. Approximate height is 4¼in (11cm). | $10-$20 |
| Tin School Bus with "Tips" | Binney & Smith | 1999 | Yellow tin bus with "Tips" waving from windows, a school fundraiser item. Front of tin can be removed. Moving wheels. Approximately 3in x 7¼in x 4in (8cm x 19cm x 10cm). | $10-$20 |
| Crayola® Time Capsule | Binney & Smith | 1999 | Huge round yellow tin is a time capsule "Tip" with clocks. Height is 7½in (19cm). | $20-$30 |

| ITEM | MANUFACTURER | YEAR | DESCRIPTION | ESTIMATED VALUE |
|---|---|---|---|---|
| Crayola® Christmas Tin | Binney & Smith | 1999 | Looks like the Christmas 1992 square tin. Children under tree, but is dated 1999. 6in x 6in x 2¾in (15cm x 15cm x 7cm). | $15-$20 |
| North American Wild Animals Limited Edition No. 1 | Binney & Smith | 2000 | Small tin with hinged top features blue "Tip" with raccoon in hat. Distributed in Australia. 1½in x 3¾ in x 4in (4cm x 10cm x 10cm). | $5-$10 |
| Bugs Limited Edition No. 6 | Binney & Smith | 2000 | Small tin with hinged top features purple "Tip" with butterfly net. Distributed in Australia. 1½in x 3¾in x 4in (4cm x 10cm x 10cm). | $5-$10 |
| Crayola® and Dole Fun Shapes | Hallmark/Dole Binney & Smith | 2000 | "Box of Imagination" includes markers, Construction Paper™ crayons, Model Magic® and ideas for using them. 6in x 3½in x 4in (15cm x 9cm x 10cm). | $15-$20 |
| Scattered Crayola® Crayons Tin | Hallmark Binney & Smith | 2000 | Large rectangular tin has crayons on lid with pastels and hot pink around sides. 7in x 10in x 3in (18cm x 25cm x 8cm). | $10-$20 |
| Crayola® Bank Tin | Hallmark Binney & Smith | 2000 | Bank tin includes 64 Crayola® crayons in box with "Tip" and friends opening a millennium vault full of money. 2½in x 6in x 6¼in (6cm x 15cm x 16cm). | $10-$15 |
| Crayola® Gold Medal | Hallmark Binney & Smith | 2000 | Flat tin with hinged side is replica of 1903 tin (No. 8). Sold in United States by Cracker Barrel. 4½in x 3¾in x 3/8in (12cm x 10cm x .9cm). | $5-$10 |
| Crayola® Millennium | Hallmark Binney & Smith | 2000 | Tin shows photographs of children from around the world and reads "Celebrate the Millennium with Crayola®." Sides have crayon boxes from 1903, 1933, 1948 and 1998. 6in x 6in x 2¾in (15cm x 15cm x 7cm). | $10-$15 |
| "Draw What?" | Binney & Smith | 2000 | A Crayola® drawing charades game in large yellow tin. 10½in x 10½in x 2¾in (27cm x 27cm x 7cm). | $10-$15 |
| Crayola®-opoly Game | Binney & Smith | 2000 | A Crayola® Monopoly-style game in large yellow tin. 10½in x 10½in x 2¾in (27cm x 27cm x 7cm). | $15-$20 |
| Crayola® Factory Land Game | Binney & Smith | 2000 | A Crayola® color matching game in large yellow tin. 10½in x 10½in x 2¾in (27cm x 27cm x 7cm). | $15-$20 |
| Crayola® Christmas Tin | Hallmark Binney & Smith | 2001 | Crayola® 2001 holiday bank tin with hinged top, features holiday scene on the front and a historical Crayola® print advertisement on the back. 2½in x 6in x 6¼in (6cm x 15cm x 16cm). | $10-$15 |

## Category: VEHICLES

| ITEM | MANUFACTURER | YEAR | DESCRIPTION | ESTIMATED VALUE |
|---|---|---|---|---|
| Crayola® Van | Corgi Binney Smith | 1986 | Yellow van with green lettering and moving wheels, made in Great Britain. 1:64 scale. | $10-$15 |
| Crayola® Delivery Car Bank | Binney & Smith | circa 1990s | Yellow and green delivery car is a bank. "Crayola® 1903 Limited Edition." | $15-$20 |
| Crayola® Tractor Trailer | Binney Smith | 1992 | Bright yellow die-cast cab with yellow plastic trailer with moving wheels. "Crayola® 1992 Edition." 1:64 scale. | $10-$20 |
| School Bus Crayola® Crayon Holder | Binney & Smith | 1993 | Bright yellow plastic Crayola® school bus is a holder for twenty-four crayons. Wheels move and clear plastic roof removes for easy access to crayons. | $10-$20 |
| 1903 Replica Train® Crayon Holder | Binney & Smith | 1994 | Dark green plastic replica of 1903 train engine is a holder for twenty-four Crayola® crayons. Wheels move and lid removes for easy access to crayons. | $10-$20 |
| Jeep Crayola® Crayon Holder | Binney & Smith | 1994 | Dark green plastic Crayola® Jeep is a holder for twenty-four crayons. Wheels move and roof removes for easy access to crayons. | $15-$25 |
| Crayola® Crayon Activity Train Set | Lionel Binney & Smith | 1994 | Lionel 11813 Crayola® Activity Train Set includes track and transformer. | $50-$75 |

156

| ITEM | MANUFACTURER | YEAR | DESCRIPTION | ESTIMATED VALUE |
|------|-------------|------|-------------|-----------------|
| Crayola® Tractor Trailer | Binney Smith | 1994 | Yellow die-cast cab with green plastic trailer with moving wheels. "Crayola® 1994 Edition." 1:64 scale. | $15-$20 |
| Crayola® Factory Tractor Trailer | Binney Smith | circa 1996 | White die-cast cab and trailer with moving wheels. "Crayola® Factory." 1:64 scale. | $40 |
| Crayola® Tractor Trailer | Revell Binney Smith | 1998 | Yellow die-cast cab and plastic trailer with moving wheels. "Crayola® Crayons 98." 1:64 scale. | $30 |
| 1998 Replica NASCAR Binney & Smith Racing Stock Car | Revell Binney Smith | 1998 | Racing stock car replica of a Sam Bass designed Chevrolet Monte Carlo. Bright yellow with green trim and Binney & Smith decals, moving wheels and hood that opens. 1:24 scale. | $20-$25 |
| 1998 Replica NASCAR Crayola® Racing Stock Car | Revell Binney Smith | 1998 | Racing stock car replica of a Sam Bass designed Chevrolet Monte Carlo. Bright yellow with Crayola® decals, moving wheels and hood that opens. 1:64 scale. | $10-$15 |
| 1937 Chevy Cabriolet Coin Bank | Liberty Binney & Smith | 1998 | Limited Edition replica 1937 Chevy Cabriolet Coupe is a lockable bank with key! Heavy die-cast metal with authentic details like running boards, headlamps, chrome grille, spare wheel cover and a jump seat with a surprise coin slot. 6½in x 2½in (17cm x 6cm). | $40 |
| 1940 Replica Ford Pedal Driven Car | Gearbox Binney & Smith | 1998 | Yellow and green convertible has colorful Crayola® crayons on trunk with moving wheels. Approximately 4in (10cm). | $5-$10 |
| 1956 Replica Ford Fairlane Pedal Driven Car | Gearbox Binney & Smith | 1998 | Red and white convertible has colorful Crayola® crayons on trunk with moving wheels. Doors say "There is only one Crayola®." Approximately 4in (10cm). | $5-$10 |
| 1957 Replica Chevy Bel Air Pedal Driven Car | Gearbox Binney & Smith | 1998 | Yellow and white convertible with moving wheels has Crayola® logo on trunk and colorful crayons on each side of car. Approximately 4in (10cm). | $5-$10 |
| 1957 Replica Chevy Bel Air Pedal Driven Car | Gearbox Binney & Smith | 1998 | Yellow and white convertible with moving wheels has Crayola® logo on trunk and colorful crayons on each side of car. Approximately 4in (10cm). | $5-$10 |
| Replica of a 1903 Delivery Car Crayola® Series #1 | Gearbox Binney & Smith | 1998 | Die-cast bank is yellow and green with Crayola® logo, has moving Goodyear tires. Limited Edition. | $10-$20 |
| Replica of a 1912 Delivery Car Crayola® Series #2 | Gearbox Binney & Smith | 1998 | Die-cast bank is yellow and green with 1903 Crayola® box and logo on each side, has moving Goodyear tires. Limited Edition. | $10-$20 |
| Replica of a 1912 Delivery Car Crayola® Series #3 | Gearbox Binney & Smith | 1998 | Die-cast bank is yellow and green with Crayola® logo and No. 8 on each side and has moving Goodyear tires. Limited Edition. | $10-$20 |
| Crayola® Tractor Trailer Truck | Revell Binney Smith | 1998 | Die-cast metal semi tractor is yellow and green with plastic split wheel drop-bed racing hauler trailer; 50th anniversary of NASCAR. 1:64 scale. | $10-$20 |
| Crayola® Crayon 1917 Sopwith Pup Airplane | Gearbox Binney & Smith | 1999 | Crayola® Limited Edition is made of heavy die-cast metal. Includes 1903 Crayola® box logo on each wing and has wingspan of 10in (25cm) | $35-$50 |
| Customized HO Train Set | Eckerd | 2001 | Electric train includes a yellow Crayola® boxcar. | $20-$30 |

**Author's Note:** As with any reference guide on collectibles, there are many old and new Crayola® items that have not been included in this book. Many of the new items, such as electronic games and toys, software and numerous varieties of Crayola® crayon boxes, can be found on the Internet and in department stores everywhere. It would be impossible to include every single item in existence. Hopefully, this book will provide readers with helpful information as they begin or add to their Crayola® collections. Good luck and happy hunting!

# References and Sources

*Art Educationist, The.* (Formerly *The Drawing Teacher.*) Editor: Clyde C. Clack. New York: Binney & Smith. 1949 to 1953. Various issues.

Binney & Smith. *The Art of Crayola® Painting.* New York: 1904

Binney & Smith. Various in-house publications such as brochures, booklets and catalogs including *The Rainbow Reporter*.

*Drawing Teacher, The.* New York: Binney & Smith. 1935 to 1948. Various issues.

Jaffee, J. "Remember Your First Crayons?" *Toy Shop Magazine.* Issue date unavailable.

Smithsonian Institution, Archives Center, Washington, D.C. Binney & Smith, Inc., Records, 1897 to 1998.

Web sites:
    http://americanhistory.si.edu/archives/d8624a.htm
    www.art4sale.com
    www.binney-smith.com
    www.Crayola.com
    www.ebay.com

# About the Author

Bonnie Rushlow was born and raised in Atlanta, Georgia. She received her B.S. in Elementary Education from Middle Tennessee State University; her M.A. in Art Education from the University of South Carolina; and her Ed.D. in Art Education from The University of Georgia.

Dr. Rushlow is currently the principal of Oakway Middle School in Westminster, South Carolina. She continues to stay active in arts education initiatives, serving on the board of the National Art Education Association as the National Director-Elect for the Supervision & Administration Division.

Bonnie has <u>always</u> loved Crayola® crayons! She began collecting Crayola® memorabilia as an elementary art teacher over 20 years ago. Her personal collection features close to 1,000 Binney & Smith items and fills several rooms in her home in Seneca, South Carolina.

Bonnie and her husband, Ken, a retired school administrator, have two grown daughters, Whitney and Courtney, who both live in Nashville, Tennessee.

The author's award from Binney & Smith for her leadership and partnership in art education.

# About the Photographer

Courtney Rushlow graduated from Middle Tennessee State University in 2001 with a Mass Communications degree in Recording Industry Management. She has worked as the coordinating producer for *Face the Music Video* on Country Music Television (CMT) in Nashville, and is currently a free-lance photographer and videographer.

The author's personalized South Carolina license plate.

# Index